Quest for Presence:
Experience and Praise

My results from the Quest for Presence Inventory caused me to be curious about the attributes of the other Attractions. As I read, I realized threads from each and every Attraction are woven through my journey with time leaving me to ask just one question, where am I being drawn to next? If you feel that time is rarely on your side, *Quest for Presence Book 3—The Attractions* may provide you with the tools and insights to become more aware and present to the preciousness of your own life's unfolding; the true gift of time.

—Kelley A. Russell-DuVarney, MA, PCC;
Resilience and Leadership Coach

Being at peace with time is essential to being a great coach, therapist, or human helper and communicator of any kind. At the core of our helping skills are the patience, presence, and awareness that lead to effective pacing of our interaction and create the space for discovery. 'Presence' is often ill-defined in the helping professions, yet this *how-to-be* part of our work is of far more value than our what-to-do part. Dr. Bennett's exploration of time and presence can open one to a way of being that is transformative for both the helper and those being helped.

—Michael Arloski, PhD, PCC, NBC-HWC; CEO,
Real Balance Global Wellness

Through *Quest for Presence Book 3—The Attractions,* Joel once again draws us deeper into the matrix unfolding around us and enfolding within us, allowing our eyes to see into the mystery of this happening life and adding hunger for every moment we have.

—Melanie Wild

Opening to a new understanding of time may be unsettling at first, especially as you orient to the new vocabulary, try to conceptualize the multidimensional forces at work, and fend off your resistance. Know that these are all part of the *Quest for Presence* journey. In this QfP volume, find your "time personality" by exploring how your way of being reveals your Attraction to a particular way of experiencing time. Slow down and ponder the text, engage with the contemplations, and notice what arises for you. Trust the parts of you that resonate with the descriptions of each Attraction, for we experience them all in different contexts and phases of life. Tune into your sense of curiosity, any stirring of memories, or your sense of fascination and awe. Using a combination of science, spiritual teachings, and personal vignettes, Dr. Joel Bennett offers fellow Questers nonjudgmental, thoughtful guidance to help us understand ourselves through a new concept of time.

—Sue Hansen, Writer/Editor/Quester; Duck Sauce Life, LLC

With wisdom and encouragement, *The Attractions* provides a magnetic pull to get curious, lean in, and open yourself up to something magical that you did not yet know was there. You discover new worlds and an awareness of a time-weaving community to support what you may be feeling or just beginning to feel. Joel and this book are a warm presence, one that welcomes and sees each part of you, a presence that gifts you the opportunity to really look within. And so, you gain a new awareness as you move toward your unique attraction in this journey called life.

Regardless of where you are in your journey, there is a gift within the Quest for Presence collection for you to discover if you feel any internal pull, curiosity, or nudge. I have read *Book 3*, twice now, in two very different seasons of life. Going through the concepts and contemplations allowed me to see where I was in my personality at that moment in time, take the next moment to settle into that vantage point, and then choose which next actions were most aligned with my heart, soul, and "attraction" (as defined in the book).

But what was most fun and interesting? With everything that was held in my journey between the two seasons of my life, and through reading and taking the Quest for Presence Inventory, I found my results provided almost identical results (*Crafting* and *Synthesizing*). I was immediately reminded of the value of awareness. I stopped and really *took the time* to look at what these results meant for me in general, in my current situations, and—most importantly—what shifts were available inside and outside the recommendations of the book. What am I being drawn to? What does attract me?

The gift of awareness and empowerment are priceless—and I believe and have witnessed the gift of its presence, which helped me settle deeper into my own unique presence.

—Briane Agostinelli, Coach, Consultant, Reiki Practitioner

In my decades as a psychotherapist, I often thought that my ability to be fully present with my clients was my therapeutic superpower. For me, being present in the here and now is essential to careful attention, deep empathy, and effective interventions. It has contributed to remarkable moments in which my clients suddenly woke up to their immediate surroundings and situations, experiencing their lives more vividly and with a clarity they had previously been missing. I think of my best work as a collaborative effort to create a sacred space in which ordinary time was irrelevant, allowing my clients' worlds to suddenly shift onto new paths.

In the world outside my work as a therapist, I have come to see presence as similarly indispensable to a satisfying life. I must be present to my experiences to manifest meaningful connections and pursue my purpose. Without presence, I float, disengaged, through time.

I am happy to have Joel Bennett as a colleague, wellness mentor, and friend. His education and experience, enthusiasm, wide-ranging intellect, and wholehearted embrace of life make for lively conversations and frequent flashes of insight. Our interactions often inhabit that electric instant of the eternal present in which I feel fully alive with him, marveling at the beauty of existence. I say all of this because Joel has a remarkable ability to translate the experience of being present with him to the page.

As I have been reading the Quest for Presence collection, I am brought again and again to the here and now rather than being transported to another time and place. I have read the books slowly, engaging with the ideas and participating in the exercises, returning repeatedly to the present. To have a book come alive and invite me to be engaged with it in the present instant is a unique experience for me. In the process, my understanding and appreciation for presence have evolved and deepened.

In these books, Joel explores the connection between being fully present to our lives and truly appreciating time. He demonstrates that, when we are truly here *now*, time ceases to be fleeting. He takes us on a journey to rediscover ourselves. He offers new perspectives on the soul, personality, and the forces shaping our lives so we may directly experience a deeper sense of the eternal, even as we are reading. On the way, he weaves insights from disparate traditions, religions, philosophy, art, and science, along with helpful maps, contemplations, and personal stories.

And through it all, he is extraordinarily present in his writing. He is fully engaged with us, heart and mind, sharing his awareness but also discovering new understandings along the way. It is a journey with the best kind of guide, one who knows the territory but is still open to the awe around him, taking pleasure in the ever-unfolding moment. He's along for the ride, not just lecturing his readers.

I encourage anyone reading this to join with Joel, me, and all the others who are accompanying him on this quest.

—Dan Jolivet, Workplace Possibilities Practice Consultant

Quest
for
PRESENCE

BOOK 3

THE ATTRACTIONS

Joel B. Bennett, PhD
Foreword by Emily Sadowski, PhD

ORGANIZATIONAL WELLNESS AND LEARNING SYSTEMS

QUEST FOR PRESENCE MANDALA

The Radiant Forces

| Form | Chaos | Nurturing Conditions | Time Shaping |

The Soulful Capacities

 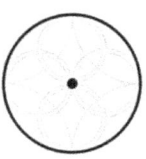  

Acceptance   Presence   Flow   Synchronicity

The Attractions

Crafting Potentiating Discerning Synthesizing Centering Coordinating Intending Catalyzing Opening

The Trajectories

Transcendence —— ... —— Interruption

Rhythm —— ... —— Pacing

Timing —— ... —— Routine

Transition —— ... —— Scheduling

The Treasures

Start here and flow clockwise

← Spontaneity → Momentousness → Fulfillment → Clutch →
Optimism → Effortlessness → Ordinariness → Coherence →
Adoration → Resonance → Patience → Preciousness →
Savoring → Poignance → Release → Awe → Spontaneity →

Published by

Organizational Wellness and Learning Systems

FLOWER MOUND, TX

Editing by Candace Johnson, Change It Up Editing, Inc.; and
Sue Hansen, Duck Sauce Life, Inc.

Cover & interior by Gary A. Rosenberg • www.thebookcouple.com
Mandala art by author, Jeffrey McQuirk, and Rob Supan

Our very nature is distinctiveness . . .
Not your thinking, but your being, is distinctiveness.

Not after difference, must ye strive;
but after YOUR OWN BEING.

At bottom, therefore, there is only one striving,
namely, the striving after your own being.

~C. G. JUNG
SEPTUM SERMONES AD MORTUOS (1916)
{SERMO I}

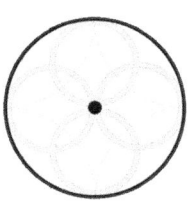

Quest for Presence Collection

The Connoisseur of Time: An Invitation to Presence

BOOK 1. *The Map and Radiant Forces*

BOOK 2. *The Soulful Capacities*

BOOK 3. *The Attractions*

BOOK 4. *The Trajectories*

BOOK 5. *The Treasures and Destiny*

Quest for Presence: Contemplations Workbook

. . . so that you ever move in the direction of bringing out your essence or deeper nature.

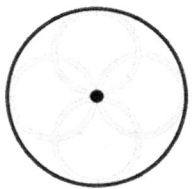

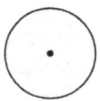

Contents

Foreword   xv

Author Note   xxi

Introduction to All Books   1

Introduction to Book 3: *Your Attraction to the Quest*   3

Part One.   Enfoldings: The Personality

Chapter 1. Insights on Personality   11

   Contemplation (QfP 3-1): Intuition, Mystery, and You   27

Chapter 2. Finding Your Bearings   29

   *Contemplation (QfP 3-2): Stop Reading, and Go
   with Your Gut*   49

Chapter 3. The Nine Attractions   51

   *Contemplation (QfP 3-3): Gaze at Your Map,
   Study It, Revise It*   85

Part Two.   The Folds: Details and Examples

Chapter 4. Portraits   89

   Contemplation (QfP 3-4): Plan, Act, Repeat   100

Chapter 5. Work and Play in the Attraction Matrix   101

   Contemplation (QfP 3-5): Your Life as a Canvas   108

Chapter 6. Relationships   111

   Contemplation (QfP 3-6): The Other   117

Chapter 7. An Attraction to a Path   119

Appendix. Using the QFPI™ with Workplace Teams   141

Key Terms   145

Research Notes   149

Acknowledgments   165

About the Author   171

Foreword

Joel Bennett and I met through synchronicity, as anyone familiar with this Quest for Presence work might expect. Joel had an intuitive hit that he was self-aware and courageous enough to follow up. And I am so glad he did.

As it turns out, we are kindred philosophers. Without knowing each other's work, we have traveled parallel intellectual journeys, contributing to an emergent perspective on living life well. This perspective helps us relate to the moment-to-moment unfolding experience of being alive. An unfolding that includes context (our whole time here), resonance (what we vibe with), and making space (and time) for our multidimensional selves.

Joel and I write about concepts so complex that most of us do not often encounter coherent writing about them. Concepts that encourage us to understand our human selves as influenced by—and influencing—unseen, metaphysical, spiritual forces. Humans are ever-evolving and becoming in a participatory, entangled cosmological context.

In an age of information (and, let us be honest, *mis*information), we sincerely need clarity. We so desperately need a language for those nondiscursive experiences—difficult-to-conceptualize ideas that help orient and ground us in our own lives, complex and uncertain as they may be. But also, in a digital age of ideation, perhaps we need a break from concepts. We need guidance and direction that nourishes our subjective experience of being and remember what it feels like to be. *Quest for Presence* helps fill both these needs. Yes, Joel accomplishes this with concepts and through many practices (contemplations), assessments, stories, and more.

Concepts allow us to trust our inner core and what we resonate with. Such trust is essential when we align to something unexpected, unconventional, nonrational, or incongruent with the person we think we are. Knowing our inner core is so important in a culture that reinforces a single or surface identity, clinging to a view of ourselves as being only one way (a personality trait, a type, a character profile).

Such a culture mainly educates and rewards analytic, logical, linear, and goal-directed thinking. It sends messages—through consumerism, media, and glorification of personal achievement—that promote the illusion of separateness. It inculcates in us a relationship with time where we mostly exploit time to our 'advantage' in the mission to 'get things done'—no matter the cost.

But conceptualizing oneness is a funny goal. As a spiritual awareness, oneness is not something you can think about or ponder. It must be experienced. As Joel has written, "We cannot think our way into presence; we can only feel our way into presence."

To feel into presence, the framework in *Quest for Presence Book 3—The Attractions* helps us connect to those unseen forces that shape our experience of life and our time on Earth. As the Introduction states, "It is easier for us to discern our attractions when we have a language for oneness." So, readers receive a recurring invitation for both self-awareness and self-transcendence. The framework—the QfP mandala—helps us experience our whole selves. And yet a framework alone is not enough to change our experience of time, ourselves, and life. We need to do the work—to feel into the unfolding.

Another point of connection between our bodies of work is a not-so-secret agenda of inviting the reader into the *moreness* of life, to include spirituality in all our self-inquiry, since in a sense, for both of us, all of life is a spiritual practice. In my case, I sometimes say that writing about intuition is a ruse for writing about consciousness more generally. As Joel says, thinking about time often ushers us into thinking about transpersonal, self-transcendent themes. In other words,

Joel and I share a commitment to wholeness. Wholeness, which is another way of understanding healing, requires our awareness. As seekers of wholeness, we must know ourselves and our world through a transpersonal lens.

Quest for Presence is so much deeper and more meaningful than most typologies—especially those used in professional, academic, and even self-help spaces. Joel invites us in a personal way, a prism of understanding who we are and why we are. At the same time as raising inspiring spiritual, existential questions, he offers an introspective path to letting those questions inform and enhance our lives. For example, the experience of reading through the nine Attractions can become a journey in resonance—what fits with who I am now? What is emerging in my life? What is happening beneath the surface of my daily life?

Practicing resonance (turning intuitively into one's evolution)—what a radical shift from traditional approaches to self-assessment! I love how Joel has taken psychological assessment and personality inventories to this new place; reimagining these within a framework that accommodates nonlinear development, uncertainty, nuance, soulful intuition, and the reality of multidimensional experience. The QfP inventory encourages you to bring your whole self to your work and to all relationships (including the relationship with your self). Humans are organic, multidimensional beings, after all. It only makes sense to seek to know ourselves by allowing us to be all the possible ways we can show up to life—all at the same time. Life is a process, not a category.

Weaving theory, practice, poetry, and contemplation, *Quest for Presence Book 3* helps us navigate process, relationships, and how we spend our days (work and play alike). As Joel reminds us, the map is not the terrain. But a map helps us orient. In the stories he shares from his own psychospiritual journey, maps play a pivotal role. Like Tarzan's vines, we can hold one map or framework until another is within grasp. That is not to say the map we have left also leaves us. In this age of secular spirituality, we can be imprinted by many maps—even many at once.

Being in a culture with many choices can lead us to hold too lightly—to try the next best thing, to treat spiritual growth like a child in a candy store—rather than dwell longer in the discomfort that often comes with perseverance and commitment. We discard what would take us deeper when it feels challenging or even just deep. Sometimes, that happens just before the transformation. Again, trust is required as we surrender to the flow of time and allow ourselves to be present.

But Joel wisely anticipates this. In the invitation to retake the inventory and sit with ourselves regularly, we are invited to keep revisiting "our time" when the terrain has shifted—whether in a new job, a new phase of life, or a new phase of the unfolding of our being. Throughout our lifelong evolution, the map is a talisman of shared experience and our potential. Our attraction to the future is an ongoing attraction to our destiny.

There is no shortage of self-development tools we can turn to. But the contemplations and tools in *Quest for Presence Book 3* provide a self-awareness strategy that does not simply take us out of our lives to look at it. It does not ask us to be something we are not. Nor does it expect us to be static in our self-expression and self-understanding. Instead, it includes a wide variety of suggestions about how to receive ourselves—as we are, again and again.

With an expansiveness that reminds me of the philosopher Henri Bergson, *The Attractions* guides us to learn about ourselves through thinking about our experience of the 4th dimension, to contemplate how we shift, change, evolve, and unfold over time. As we learn to trust our unfolding, our attractions, and desires, we can allow ourselves to be what we are.

Joel says this is not a book about big, evolutionary ideas, but I beg to differ. As he writes, this book aims "to help you develop an awareness of unfolding" a self that is interdependent with others, the world, and the cosmos. The process of emergence, of witnessing the unfolding of who we are—even though it's happening on the personal level—is evolutionary work on a more significant human scale. When more of us share our unfolding, we will more likely change time (beyond the clock), rather than only view time as changing us. Our planet needs this.

Time is the context in which you are invited to explore the QFPI inventory, its archetypes (the Attractions), our thoughtful alignment, and ultimate resonance with healthy, whole time—an array of opportunities for introspection. It is so liberating to consider a dynamic notion of the self beyond fixed ego, a metapersonal construal of oneself.

I cannot help but think of QfP in relation to a Buddhist koan, the question: Who were you before you were born? This book is an invitation to strip away layers of our conditioning. Like a lotus, we unfold, layer upon layer, to uncover a seed self and all the creative potential within.

Dr. Emily Sadowski, PhD
Toronto, Ontario
January 2024
Visit www.emilysadowski.com

Author Note

Quest for Presence, or *QfP* for short, includes five books. Each can be read independently or as part of the whole; they need not be read in sequence. If you are just entering the collection, welcome! Your journey begins with *QfP Book 3: The Attractions*.

QfP is written and structured to support your sense that the particular book you are reading is just right for you. Indeed, the notion of time in *QfP* is about being wherever you happen to be.

Readers of *QfP* like that it has a "choose your own adventure" quality, offering a variety of entry points for engaging with core concepts. If you are new to these topics, I recommend that you read straight through each book. Please pause to review the contemplations at the end of most chapters (or complete corresponding activities in the *QfP Contemplations Workbook*, or both). It will help to read my personal reflections, as they illustrate how these concepts render in real life.

Each book also comes with notes in a research notes section, many of which relate to the science of time or provide references for readers interested in the related concept in the text. *QfP* is informed by a vast literature in the growing study and philosophy of time. However, these books are not intended to be evidence-based or academic. I am not summoning research to advance a new science of presence. I hope you will explore these notes only when your curiosity outweighs your desire to achieve time competency.

By time competency, I mean the ability to return to living in the present moment of your whole life (staying "on script," as it were).

There are two steps to being time competent. First, you notice when anxiety, worry, longing, or overthinking (your mental future) pull you away from the adventure; or when regret, remorse, self-judgment, or ruminations (your mental past) push you out of the moment. Second, you gently return to the here and now and the feeling that your whole-time is a happening, unfolding, or awesome life journey.

If you are re-entering the collection by way of another starting point, I invite you to reconnect to your journey. As is the nature of any quest, wherever you are along your path—and whichever book you find yourself reading—there you are.

The title of this book changed often as it went into final edits. This dynamic is a contemplation in itself. Does the way a book appears—judging a book by its title—make any difference to how you arrived here? I have listed the titles below. I think they all work. But the world requires us to fix things into a lasting word or image. I hope you find one that resonates with you.

A Quest for Presence, This Happening Life, Time's Precious Weave, Your Journey of Wholeness, Finding Free Time This Whole Time, Recovering Time in a World Addicted to Distraction and *Contemplations for Your Whole Time Here.*

* * *

I encourage you to download a free copy of the preview to QfP on our website www.presencequest.life. *The Connoisseur of Time: An Invitation to Presence* has helped many get a solid grasp of the reason for this journey. You will also find resources and events on our site to support you in your quest.

ABOUT THE ABBREVIATION Q*f*P

The *f* symbol between Q and P (a letter f with a descender hook) is the notation used in mathematics to represent functions. Specifically, functions represent how a varying quantity depends on another quantity. For example, the position of a planet is a function of time, or a weekly salary is a function of the hourly pay rate and the number of hours worked, or supply is a function of demand: As price goes up, demand goes down. In our quest for presence, our journey is a function of our presence, and at the same time, our presence is a function of our journey. As you become more present, the experience of life as a happening adventure and unfoldment is more enhanced. As your experience of life enhances, you become more present. The thrill is in the ride, and the ride is in the thrill.

Introduction to All Books

To be present means to be present to the whole-time of your life. Being here now is important. Equally important is your whole life—where you came from and where you are headed. We just don't live in the now. Our whole life is a project of purpose and meaning, a coming into being, a path of sense-making, a place where everything fits together, a journey, a becoming, an arrival, a fulfillment of destiny, a momentous emergence, a cause, a calling, an awakening, and so much more. And all of these occur outside of "clock-time."

Presence happens when we show up and fully engage in this life with all its changes, interruptions, and distractions. Our presence is imperfect. This collection of books encourages you to embrace its imperfections. Our attention faces many challenges: advertisements, attention deficit, abuse, anxiety, aging, and cognitive decline, to name a few. Life is fleeting, a blur. How can you find the time to live it and live it well? Perhaps it's time to embrace the blur of your whole-time here.

This Quest for Presence (QfP) collection is designed to help you reach any number of objectives. This includes the actual letting go of specific deadlines in favor of contemplations that improve your presence. This idea may seem radical in a society oriented toward action, achievement, and accomplishment. As you will discover, this orientation is born out of a narrow-minded, fragmenting, and dysfunctional view that time comprises only "clock-time." A different, contemplative objective would be that you stop long enough to enjoy the rich, full, and precious aspects of this very brief life.

The QfP is about making room for uplifts, for positive moments, for glimpses of the amazing wonders and emotions that life has to offer. I call these *Treasures*. My hope is that you will become more inquisitive about these Treasures. Where do they come from? How can you experience them more frequently? Are you prone to experiencing certain kinds more than others? Through the QfP, I believe you will get answers to these questions. Your view of time will change. You will have more well-being, wholeness, and intimacy in your life—both with others and with the ever-evolving natural world.

Other objectives stem from these questions. A new perspective may help you be more efficient. To value your time in a new way may give you the motivation and tools to prioritize what matters most. Alternatively, as you discover the big picture of time—as delineated here—you may grow in your sense of spirituality, faith, and transcendence of life's problems. My personal aim for you lies in between these two areas: efficiency and spirituality. This happens by embracing the ordinariness of life by becoming present to it.

Whatever your troubles, a shared presence can also make you resilient and thrive. This quest for presence is meant to be shared. We have arrived here as conscious beings because of cosmic forces that modern physics has only begun to understand. Deterioration of intimacy is the greatest problem of time compression (see my book *Time and Intimacy: A New Science of Personal Relationships* [Erlbaum, 2000]). We cannot appreciate our time without each other. As such, this offering is also a memoir. I hope you get to know me well enough so you feel less alone and more connected. And since we are here, we might as well make the most of it. Together.

Introduction to Book 3: Your Attraction to the Quest

Each of us has a human sense of an individual self, an awareness of some identity (our own being) that continues through time. Your perception of your distinctive "self" and your sense of time are woven together. On the one hand, let go of the self (of having to *be* somebody), and time evaporates. On the other hand, enrich and deepen your wise sense of time—the precious weave of this happening life, and the self blossoms and flourishes.

Philosophers have long examined the relationship between our sense of self and our understanding of time. These topics are the focus of ongoing studies in the sciences of behavior and psychology. I throw my hat into this ring in the hope that you, dear reader, can milk your awareness of *your self in time* for all it is worth. That which you consider yourself to be "you" is actually an exquisitely complex, unique, and dynamic pattern. "You" are an unfolding of traces, threads, forces, and fields from beyond that have come together to create what you perceive as your "awareness." Author Philip Roth writes in his novel *Indignation*,

> I'm interested in what people do with the chaos in their lives and how they respond to it, and simultaneously what they do with what they feel like are limitations. If they push against these limitations, will they wind up in the realm of chaos, or will they push against limitations and wind up in the world of freedom?

We all have both chaos and limitations in our lives, and we also have compulsions that can betray us and regrets for missed opportunities. As Roth implies, what matters is how we respond to the situation of our lives. And there is more. It is also essential to look for the pattern—across the chaos, limitations, compulsions, and opportunities—and discern what attracts us, moves us forward, and brings us to the present. Our story unfolds every day. When we cultivate a deeper awareness of that unfolding, we wind up in the world of freedom.

First, our memory powers an ability to take ourselves as the single thread in the unfolding story, the successive frames of this happening life. Second, our experience of our self as something unique and distinct from others, otherwise referred to as "personality," also maintains a continued *presence* through the stories we tell about our own life. This presence is more than a mental faculty. As explained in *QfP Book 2*, Presence is a Soulful Capacity. Along with Acceptance, Flow, and Synchronicity, we have the tools we need to explore, to plumb the depths of our very existence—the purpose and meaning of our story.

Many spiritual teachers use the metaphor of the soul as a needle, ever pointing toward the magnet of its universal origin: unity, oneness, God, the Great Spirit. We want to go back to our home. Saints and gurus guide that needle toward its attraction. However, our direct experience of the timeless soul is fleeting, difficult, and seemingly impossible. Many who walk a spiritual path—especially without a guide—face a huge gulf between the first awakening of their sense of soul and the return to oneness.

This is where your personal story and your experience, your feelings, of the Attractions come in. First, it is easier to discern your attractions when you have a language for oneness. Second, even with a guide, you still have to work with your own self, identity, or personality. These are closer, sort of "in your face." Third, the experience—let alone the idea—of oneness and unity can be a great challenge even when you have great faith. To help, I hypothesize that it helps to view oneness—the unity of the universe—as consisting of more identifiable cosmic forces. As this book describes, a team of magnets are always pulling at our soul or pulling at our personality to join the soul as it points toward oneness.

So, we discover something else going on beyond our memory and behind the story. Our "sensation of self" emerges from the interplay of cosmological—or Radiant—Forces. By "radiant," I mean that these forces are like rippling fields that emit power, constantly breathing in and out, expanding and collapsing like transparent spheres, each the size of a universe. These forces provide unlimited energy and freedom for our lives as a whole, and they create our experience of time in subtle but profound ways. *QfP Book 1* explains the forces in greater detail.

This *QfP Book 3* guides us to understand how these cosmological forces both unfold our story and enfold our personality within that story. In short, like magnets, we have unique Attractions to these forces. *QfP Book 3* introduces a measure of *time personality* that asks about your preference for seeing time as a function of the four Radiant Forces: Form, Chaos, Time Shaping, and Nurturing Conditions. But this book is not about personality as it is commonly defined. Instead, it is about our soulful *Attractions* to the four universal and Radiant Forces. The Quest for Presence Inventory™ (QFPI™) is designed to spark insight into your personality, specifically, how you express your presence in unique ways.

The self-assessments and contemplations in Book 3 should empower you to create a new language and orientation toward time that is more enriching and spiritual than mechanical and clock-like. The QFPI™ approach to personality—the Attractions—provides a window into your unique way of taking the presence journey. It helps you see your character in the context of the totality of time's precious weave.

You may think you are here for a short time. But I have news: Cosmic time, as you befriend it, can help you see the more extraordinary dance. And it is playing out now, so strap yourself in.

Your Starting Point

Some readers may want to jump in and take the QFPI™ in chapter 2. You can also skip to chapter 7 (An Attraction to the Path), which is my own story about the path toward developing the QFPI™. However, each chapter builds upon the others in sequence to prepare you for getting the most out of the QFPI™.

In Part One (Enfoldings: The Personality), I unpack how your life as a conscious, growth-minded human being unfolds in ways that nourish your inner being (soul, essence). I ask you to approach your understanding of your personality—the Attractions—through a growth-mindset lens. Chapter 1 clarifies the difference between personality traits and Attractions. Then, in chapter 2, you are introduced to the *Attraction Matrix* (aka the QFPI™). Before taking it, I ask you to agree to nine Attraction Matrix Commitment Statements. There are statements for each Attraction designed to help you get in touch with *your Attraction process*. Chapter 3 then presents nine feedback forms with brief interpretations of the Attractions that will help you discern your Attractions even further.

Part Two (The Folds: Details and Examples) contains examples of how the Attractions manifest. You can refer to Part Two for comparing your QFPI™ results with these examples. First, I provide several portraits of others who have taken the QFPI™ on more than one occasion and what it meant to them (chapter 4). Then, I share recent experiences of how the nine Attractions manifested in my work and home life (chapter 5) and my relationships (chapter 6). Finally, chapter 7 is autobiographical, where I trace how it all started for me and the early influences on my career that encouraged this book.

An Emerging Paradigm

As you follow this sequence through the chapters, I hope you will see that your insight into your Attractions is also an unfolding and *enfolding* journey. I ask you to put aside all previous notions about any personality classification system, such as personality traits, archetypes,

types, drives, strengths, or colors. These are remnants, artifacts, from an old view of personality. What you learn through the Q*f*P journey will accommodate not only those existing perspectives about personality but also any ideas, concepts, or theories about the nature of time that evolve from physics, quantum theory, cosmology, adult development, aging, neurology, and other sciences. Yes, a new paradigm is emerging.

To Evolve Beyond the Fixed

We are an evolving species. At least, we must evolve to address our challenges as a human species. Just because people act a certain way does not mean we have to treat them (or even ourselves) as though they have an enduring, fixed way of being. Indeed, all the teachers in my life (and I acknowledge many of them in chapter 7) treated me as though I would and could act in a new and "better" way. They did not reify me by behaving toward me in ways that confirmed my limited view of myself. It is partly because they saw potential in me that I could evolve toward more of who I was to become or who I was meant to be. I am deeply grateful for these teachers; this book is dedicated to them.

We can "de-reify" our fixed sense of who we are as a species. So let's find ways to nudge each other along. We can do this not in spite of our fixed tendencies but because of them. Your own "personality" can get a new bearing in the blur of this happening life— this new awesome, surprising, and evolving universe. The QFPI™ is a starting place or focal point to help us get these bearings in our individual and collective quest for presence. Accordingly, the tools in this book are most valuable when shared with others.

One more thing. I believe that as humanity evolves, we will come to a place where what we call "personality," at least as we know it today, will no longer be valid or serve our evolution. Of course, this does not mean we will each become exactly the same, like robots or automatons. However, it is certainly possible that we will lose our individuality and uniqueness. An overabundance of modern science fiction novels and movies portray how this will play out: excessive political control leads to dystopian totalitarianism; unbridled technology leads to artificial intelligence biohacking our brains; or a parasitic virus takes our nervous system hostage.

The fear of losing our uniqueness comes partly from believing we are fundamentally special and unique—as individuals, nations, and species. We imagine the intrepid extraterrestrial saying, "If you have seen one human being, you have seen them all."

I see it playing out differently. And, as with everything else in this Q*f*P collection, it has to do with reinventing our understanding of time. We can enhance our self-concept by freeing ourselves from fixed notions of time. We can play with and explore more dynamic ways of becoming, especially in relation to forces we are just beginning to understand through such fields as cosmology, quantum physics, and the brain sciences. And there are fields yet to evolve: quantum genetics, neurocosmology, and others. This book is not about big evolutionary ideas; it invites you to be curious and explore how you might evolve. At the very least, I hope it opens you to new ways of thinking about yourself. All ideas that change the world for the better start with the imagination and inspiration of a higher self.

The Radiant Forces break us out of the prison of clock-time. The Soulful Capacities protect us from time famine. No longer do we view time as only something to be managed or mastered. The Attractions—our own distinctive attraction to our destiny—is also our unique intelligence, our genius.

As you follow your Attraction you will move from time management to time genius . . . and ultimately discover the treasures of life that wait for your arrival.

Enfoldings:
The Personality

An Ode to Personality

Time textures you, inside and out.
Through and through.
Can you feel the edges, the folds,
and smooth and rough parts?
We all have them.

Jesus: the true outlaw;
Buddha: the jaded lamplighter;
Moses: the holiest emigrant;
Mohammed: the orphaned GuideStar.

What were *they* attracted to?
What kept *them* up at night?

They practiced meeting the Real.
They became textured in who they wholly were.
Through and holy through.

And now, there is you:
What are you attracted to?
What keeps you up at night?
Who do you want to meet?
Where, in this great swirl of holiness, is your journey?

~Joel Bennett (J.B.)

Your very being, your essence, your deepest and most soulful self, is enfolded within your personality. Your essence cannot be objectified because it sits behind all objects, including the folds of your personality. As life's blur happens, more folds occur, more definition, more detail. Every now and then, take the *time* to notice the details of who you are becoming. Sit there, with *time* and with the *unfold*, and also notice: What is it that resides within you that yearns for and enjoys the light?

CHAPTER 1

Insights on Personality

An Ode to Fanning Out

Everything in the universe is moving toward
    what each thing is attracted to.
The scientists say that the movement is the
    true measure of time.

Your soul knows that the true measure lies
    in the attraction itself.
The inner measure of everything,
your original dwelling.

Time only came to nudge you out a bit,
get you to swim about, explore.

These lines of light fan out from your den,
    then bring you back, again and again.

Be like those other galaxies,
with all their impossible colors,
tilting with abandon
at the approaching void.

~J.B.

assume you are reading this book because you are attracted to a higher state of BEING, a spiritual realm, a deeper and more sustained state of meaning and purpose, or greater clarity of your place in the world and the universe. You want more love in your life. The soul is yearning to awaken. A part of you is excited about this fleeting mystery. The question this book seeks to answer is, "What or who is the 'you' that has this Attraction?" The brief answer is that you are a complex, ever-evolving combination of, or rather a dance between, your soul essence, your personality, and the Attraction itself. Your personality is important, and it will be helpful—for now and for the purpose of this book—to distinguish it from this Attraction. There are four distinctions to be made.

Difference Between Personality and Attraction

First, whereas "personality" often refers to an outer self, persona, or mask; "attraction" refers to an inner potential. We each have a ripening tendency to be drawn to and be influenced by deeper universal forces. Indeed, as we shall learn, these forces are themselves *attractors*, alive in four-dimensional space-time. As defined here, *personality* refers to a set of traits and qualities that distinguish how a person appears unique or is characterized as unique by others. In contrast, *Attraction* refers to an evolving orientation toward our own becoming and our inward experience of time.

This experience of Attraction lives particularly outside or apart from notions (or social constructs) of clock-time. We are more than a trait assembly. Each of us is an evolving pattern. Only society, the relic of inherited social norms and rules, leads us to think otherwise. Our traits, our persona, and the masks we wear are just conventions to help us fit in, get along, learn a skill, get a job, become "somebody."

Time is not the objective hands of the ticking clock but the emergent pattern we help weave on our journey. Because of our genetic makeup, history, and experience, we tend to see this bigger picture of time in the nested and unfolding journey of our life as a whole. This tendency is not a fixed trait. It is a probability and an opportunity. Our life is an ever-changing journey of discovery, not a library book where everything can be indexed or reduced to bits or bytes of information that can be hyperlinked and accessed instantaneously via the Internet.

Feelings Constitute the Attractions

Second, our personality is distinct and feels different from our inner-self, our essence or soul. This is especially important to remember when we over-identify with specific traits, when we take ourselves to be fixed and separate from others, from nature and the cosmos. This over-identification or fixation is the basis of ego and a sense of separateness. In contrast, our Attractions are deeply rooted in the cosmos and nature. We can feel these Attractions as natural stirrings, quickenings, or inklings within our bodies and emotions. And they can be understood with and through others with similar and different attractions.

Our Attractions live closer to and are informed and enlightened by the Soulful Capacities of Acceptance, Presence, Flow, and Synchronicity (see *QfP Book* 2). Accordingly, to fully appreciate one's attraction to the cosmos, it is best to view your assessment of your Attractions (your QFPI™ results) alongside your evaluation of your Soulful Capacities (see *QfP Book* 2).

When we feel most alive, vital, and vibrant, it is often because we tap into an energy or force that lifts us beyond a fixed and separate sense of identity. We have an intuition about something greater; we not only feel a sense of self-fulfillment but of self-transcendence. This innermost and private feeling arises in any of the following ways.

✦ The thrill of being creative or taking on a challenge.

✦ The excitement for influencing a project.

✦ The sense of joy at seeing, coordinating, or engineering a pattern.

- The warmth from finding a centered space in our lives amid chaos.

- An uplift from negotiating and finding intimacy with others.

- The sense of deep love from supporting the learning or nudging the growth of others.

- The sensation of thriving within life itself.

As examples, these convey only a small range of possibilities. There is a whole other kind of feeling, often ineffable: a stirring, a quickening, a shock, being overcome, a knowing, a certainty, a rising up from within, a flash of insight, a realization, or a cleansing surge of energy. These feelings are essential in our quest for presence. We have to remember that society, clock-time, and an overfocus on Time Shaping (getting things done) and Form (showing proof that we got things done) tends to keep us from paying attention to, cultivating, and celebrating these stirrings. We also have to remember that these feelings are among the most uniquely private experiences we can have, are often profound, and often fleeting.

What Is the Purpose of Personality?

Third, most approaches to personality fail to explain human traits in the context of essence. The question "What is the purpose of my personality?" is central to the quest for presence. To be clear, many of us struggle with aspects of our ego and personality that we either don't like or consider less favorable than others. Interestingly, we consider them as "unattractive." In different paths of personal development, these are character flaws, defects, vices, addictions, compensations, blind spots, ego complexes, ego fixations, or fragments of self. Our spiritual growth depends on working with, understanding, and either overcoming or integrating these personal demons. We find our essence, our light, through the dark side and the shadow.

BOX 1.1: The Four Radiant Forces as Attractors in an "Attraction Matrix"

Imagine a large, empty space within a box. There is a magnet in each of the four corners of the box. These magnets have a magnetic force that attracts other objects and turns on and off their power at different rates and intensities. In the center of the box, a small, metallic sphere hangs in midair, held there by the magnetic forces. The sphere is seen to continually dance and gyrate because of the oscillating and varying intensities of the magnets. Sometimes it moves up. Sometimes it moves down. It also spins left and right or along different axes. At other times, it oscillates from the center to the periphery of the box and back again and again.

In addition, there is no time within the box. No clock can be referenced for when these moves might occur, how long they take, or their frequency. Everything that happens in the life of the metallic sphere appears spontaneous, as though it were happening for the first time.

This metaphor conveys how the different magnets attract the metallic sphere and that this attraction itself is how time is defined. Indeed, when all the forces are operating at the same moment, it is possible that the metallic sphere holds perfectly still within a matrix of every possible attraction—in which case, time itself stands still. Alternately, and more often, the sphere is gyrating wildly and rapidly and appears like a blur.

The four magnets each represent the four Radiant Forces. These forces exist as given, objective, and ongoing realities. Everything has—to varying degrees—Form, Chaos, Time Shaping, and Nurturing Conditions.

Form (structure, gravity). The tendency for things to remain constant, have stability and a recognizable structure and identity.

Chaos (entropy, dissipation). The tendency for things to eventually disintegrate, fall apart, and decompose. Science writer Brian Greene describes entropy in this way: "Everything in the universe has an overwhelming tendency to run down, to degrade, to wither."

Time Shaping (action, intention, cause and effect). The actual occurrence where one object or agent acts upon another object or agent such that the other is changed, impressed, or influenced or its immediately preceding trajectory has been altered. For human beings, this Time Shaping is often preceded by an intention.

Nurturing Conditions (facilitation, becoming, temporal context). The conditions that precede and surround the emergence of any phenomena such that a person, relationship, or system evolves, becomes, mutates, circulates, or otherwise changes in ways that would not be possible without those conditions.

Form

Chaos

Time Shaping

Nuturing Conditions

Each of the Attractions also comes with challenges or cautions. These challenges are caused by a limited sense of time or urgency, a need to have things proceed a certain way; or fixation on a memory such that we only see the present moment through the distorting lens of that memory. On the one hand, we may overemphasize or fixate on one Attraction as the only way to navigate our quest for presence. On the other hand, we may cloak, hide from, or ignore a more profound Attraction because it stirs up too many feelings. Further, we may judge certain Attractions because of significant others in our lives who hurt or abused us. They were "just that way," and we must not be like them. We see the judging and limited ego in each of these examples.

In their basic and inherent nature, the Attractions are an expression of the objective laws in the enduring and eternal four Radiant Forces. When we ask, "What is the purpose of my personality?" we find the answer in revealing the dance of the very forces that give rise to our unique expression in this life and on this path. The soul knows that the body is impermanent and that our ego and personality are limited. We were not born to assert and reestablish some trait or narrative simply. Instead, we are here because we are attracted to some unlimited aspect of our being and becoming.

Personality Is Not Essence

Fourth, when we tune in to what attracts us, we automatically open the gift of the moment. Accepting this gift, we become present to the occasion of our life. And, our Presence within this occasion allows us to flow with whatever unfolds next. Some examples of this can be seen in the unfolding rhythm and flow of Tai Chi or in transitions from one yoga posture to another. As we move from one stance or posture to another, our muscles automatically attune to and, moment to moment, actualize the very next posture. We are attracted to the potential space that our torso and limbs will inhabit. With sensorimotor micro-precision, we adapt and adjust into the realization of who we are.

We grow and evolve precisely because we enfold information from the anticipated and envisioned future into our nervous system. The seed of an acorn holds the entire pattern of the fully mature tree. The seed is attracted to the larger matrix of its own becoming. Our essence, all the information of who we ever were and who we could ever be, is enfolded within our personality.

Importantly, the gift of the moment is where the Treasures of life— such as love, beauty, and awe—arise. We become fully alive between life's unfoldings and the unique way we enfold the Treasures of life within our personality. In making the distinction between Attractions and personality, we don't ignore dispositions, traits, and qualities that endure. We do not throw out the personality as we might throw the baby out with the bathwater. Instead, we let the soulful nature of the Attractions bring about uplifting experiences. Treasures then season and mature the personality.

REFLECTION

I used to struggle with what important people in my life called my "neediness." My personality came across as fawning, obsequious, and just plain needy. "You wear your heart on your sleeve too much," they said. On different occasions and from different people, I was told I looked like a "lost puppy dog." Apparently, these traits were unattractive to others. I wanted to be more confident and less dependent on others. I sought out spiritual teachers to help. One person, a spirit guide who would enter into a trance, called in a deceased doctor who read one's own spirit. He said that "your soul came into the earth realm and was born too quickly. You were not ready to inhabit a human life. You have to work to fit in and be like other human beings." One Buddhist teacher told me that in a previous life, I was a young baby monkey, abandoned and left alone by my family. This life was about healing the trauma. Later on, I learned about codependence and relationship addiction and attended many 12-step groups with other struggling addicts.

The process of identifying, working through, accepting, and transforming my "neediness" took many years. I discovered that many people have the same trait, a similar wound. They need to feel loved, cared for, and to belong. I now see that the vulnerability of dependence is not a defect; it is a window into common humanity and a source of compassion. I also see a crystal-clear purpose from the journey: the people I have met, the teachers, and all the books, retreats, and other lessons I learned because of this so-called defect (see chapter 7 for more detail). My career has clearly been an opportunity to help others with their own vulnerability, especially those struggling with depression, addiction, pain, and suicidal ideation. I have created workshops, courses, and tools that break down the stigma of "neediness" and successfully encourage people to reach out.

Looking back, an aspect of my being was attracting me to a state of wisdom about my personality. We are all born with, or acquire early on, certain traits that need work—to be accepted, understood, dialed up, or dialed down. As we work on these traits, we enfold new information. At the same time, our deeper essence is folded in as well. We have a core need—to take the journey—and there is nothing wrong with needing that.

Enfolding

In your quest for presence, this happening life unfolds before you while, at the same time, you are enfolding (taking in, receiving, processing) information. The image of unfolding brings to mind how a new page turns in a storybook, the next scene develops in a theatrical play, the petals of a flower separate in the bloom, or the vista changes as we round a corner in our hike through nature. It also brings to mind how a pattern unfolds in a tapestry as it is woven on a loom.

Add your "self" to the above images, and do so as someone who is unfolding or emerging on your walk through this journey of life. In a way, you are building the bridge as you walk on it. Your self is also unfolding (verb) and you are also *an unfolding* (noun). The next page is blank until you turn it. The dialog in the next scene emerges only when your voice is added to it. You waited around long enough to see the petals unfurl. The tapestry is the very interweaving of your soul and personality. Everything has a genetic template with many, but not all, preprogrammed elements for what is probably going to happen next. How we live and journey through our life can even change our biology, the genetic template.

The enfoldings within your personal journey run counterpoint to the unfoldings. Life does not only happen to us; we also happen to life. As described above in the examples of Tai Chi and yoga, you always take information from the anticipated and envisioned future and enfold that information into your story. The template of every book is made up of successive pages that you have some inkling about within your soul. This clue may be tiny, but it is there.

Your intuition is an essential aspect of your personality that connects you to the unfolding. The template or pattern of every movie or theatrical play consists of dialog nested within scenes nested within acts. You also intuit and enfold this pattern into the Attractions of your own story as you journey forward. From every page and every scene, something *happens* that alerts you to the fact that you are alive.

While life is *unfolding* for us from one occasion to the next, your personality and consciousness enfold new information from your essence, however dimly perceived. To better understand this, another metaphor may help. Imagine the course of your life like that of making and tasting a well-seasoned soup or stew. Every occasion is an assembling of a wide variety of ingredients and spices. You carefully tend to this soup over time, folding in (enfolding) different ingredients at certain times. Your personality is the unique blend of seasoning and textures that emerges over time and gives your soup or stew a different taste from any other. This entire process—from assembling and enfolding the ingredients of each life occasion—is another way to look at your quest for presence.

This metaphor about enfolding speaks to the intuitive approach to life and is distinct from the intellective approach. Advances in science reinforce a more intellective rather than intuitive way of knowing and even present these as two distinct methods of knowing. Despite this, research shows that most people believe in a soul that receives the information and experiences both the unfolding and enfolding of life. Some call this karma; others call it destiny. Either way, we have an innermost aspect of our being that differs from opinions, ideas, attitudes, or ego and personality; something that transcends a current self or personality.

The Radiant Forces of life *act upon* us and propel us. They *unfold* our unique journey—why we are here—to the degree that our souls are ready to have them develop. These forces also *act within and through* us. Our distinct personality is made up of those same forces. The forces are *enfolded* within us in a unique pattern, unlike any other in the world. Hence, the term *enfold* has additional meanings. It is like someone enfolds us in their arms in a full embrace. Similarly, the forces embrace us along our journey. Our personality consists of layers of folds like a blanket, quilt, or drapery. Here again, we see the metaphor of a precious weave, an emerging tapestry.

An Illustration of Enfolding

The image below further conveys this idea. At the top of the graphic, one person moves toward a treasure across successive but separate frames. Imagine that this represents events unfolding over time, as you perceive them. This is how we typically think of unfolding—for example, from page to page, phase to phase, etc.

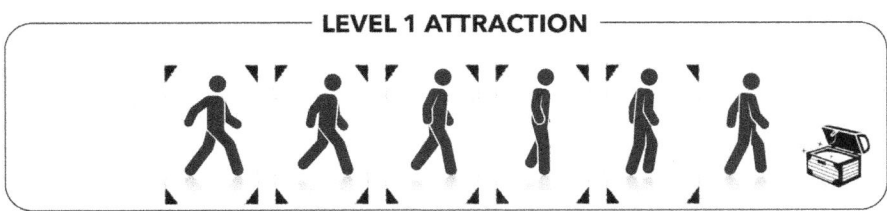

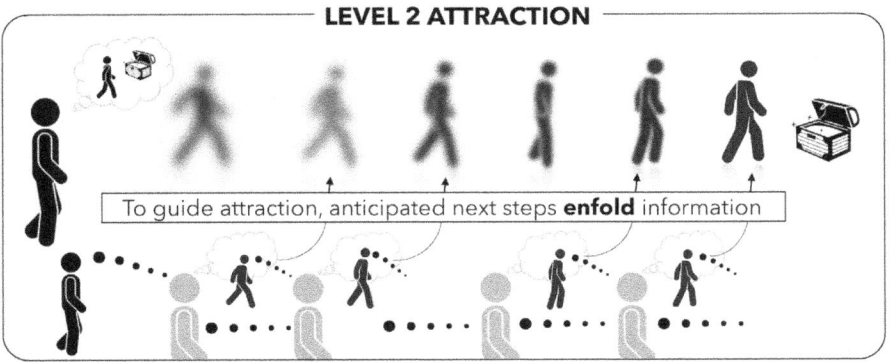

Note. The picture conveys attraction to a treasure only as an example. We can be attracted to a variety of goals or destinations, such as a place, a person, an educational degree, a vocation, or a spiritual path.

Underneath this top depiction, we see another perspective of what is happening—from the standpoint of enfolding. Look at the image on the far left of the person with the thought cloud. This cloud illustrates the person's intention to find the treasure on the far right. (They are attracted to the idea of receiving whatever lies inside the treasure box.) We also can say the person on the left is drawn to the situation or state of "possessing the treasure." Other continuous steps must unfold for the person to proceed from the current state (on the left) to the future anticipated state (on the far right).

As each step is taken, the person on the left incorporates, or enfolds, information. In other words, the person receives feedback that the previous step (the movement and angles of limbs) has been achieved, at least to some degree of success in moving toward the attractive state. This feedback allows for the individual to take the next step and then the next step until the anticipated state (of finding the treasure) is accomplished. The person is continually getting clearer and enfolding information from the very act of making a movement at each and every step.

This enfolding is required for the attraction—the treasure—to manifest, become viable, real, and actual. As the image shows, the situation gets less blurred and clearer. We live life. Each step toward our Attraction is the Attraction itself. We are ever becoming more real. In this example, the treasure is not only attractive (as in Level 1 Attraction). Instead, the ongoing clarification that comes from both unfolding and enfolding—the quest itself—is the attraction (as in Level 2 Attraction). This distinction is often captured when people say that "the journey is more important than the destination" or "living into the question has more value than getting an answer."

This book aims to help you develop an awareness of enfolding. Other authors have described this awareness as *relational knowing* and *process consciousness*. So essentially, to become aware of enfolding, we must practice seeing the self as changing in relationship with others over time and fine-tuning that perception. And it does take practice.

Level 1, Level 2, Level 3 Attractions

In the examples in the graphic above, the term *attraction* differs from how we will use it to understand personality. When something inside us is drawn to a treasure or another person (or place, situation, career, or something else), this is a *Level 1 Attraction*. At this initial point, there is no actual behavior, only a desire, a stirring, and an intention. Nothing has proceeded *in time*. At Level 1, we have fleeting thoughts about our self and the other, but there is less active and intentional thinking about what is happening.

When we actively proceed toward creating the meeting, encounter, or situation, then something occurs in linear and clock-time. We are attracted to something in the perceived, intuited, or imagined future (examples include a desire, goal, objective, outcome, or fulfillment of a plan), and we act toward that goal. *Level 2 Attraction* occurs when we feel pulled toward some future state of being. The whole process of moving and feeling toward that state is defined as a *Level 2 Attraction*. At Level 2, we become more aware of our thoughts. We begin to think and feel about ourselves as moving forward in time actively.

From this simple illustration, we can draw several parallels to this happening life and your quest for presence. First, life does not only unfold in front of you mechanically without your involvement and awareness to some extent. If this were the case, you would not have any presence. You would be a simple automaton following a predestined plan. Second, consciousness and intentionality are required to take each successive step as you get closer to some desired state.

By itself, this intentionality, your need to influence outcomes, would point to only one of the four Radiant Forces: Time Shaping (cause and effect, the call to take action). In other words, you would define your life as only consisting of moving from the past to the future. But you are much more than a sequence of cause and effect. There are other forces at work. This is further illustrated below and introduces the idea of *Level 3 Attraction*.

The image situates the same enfolding sequence above and Attraction *as occurring within and influenced by* the four Radiant Forces. We are subject to, informed by, and work with these forces at every step. More importantly, we are drawn (*attracted*) to these forces to varying degrees. To make this point as straightforward as possible, the Attraction is the *ongoing operation of the Forces in our lives*. These forces act on our personal preferences, tastes, inclinations, and personality.

To illustrate, if the person in the image were to be attracted *only* to Time Shaping, then the felt movement from the past to the future would be strictly linear. There would be no interruptions, and nothing else would influence the trajectory. Alternately, if the person were subject to *only* the force of Chaos, then there would be little chance of any enfolding or movement. The whole affair would simply fall apart.

The much more likely scenario—and this is the whole point of *the reality of our lives*—is that a variety of factors and forces are at play. For example, a previous occurrence sets the conditions in place for any movement to begin in the first place (Nurturing Conditions). Some trait, a character defect, an accident, an event, another unique piece of information or other display of personality interrupted us during the trajectory (Chaos). In addition, there are rules indicating when, where, and how the encounter occurred (Form).

The forces, as attractors, don't just draw us into the future; they also mold, shape, dissolve, integrate, create, merge, preview, rewind, expose, hide, lift, and influence the trajectory of our lives in a variety of other ways. This whole pattern of influence is what we mean by *Level 3 Attraction*. Not only is this sequence of events in motion—something else is moving us, and it is beyond time.

Something else is moving us, attracting us, and it is beyond time.

+ The change in consciousness from Level 1 to Level 2 involves having a fleeting thought of the self to actively and deliberately thinking about and feeling the self.

+ The move to Level 3 is a move more toward *knowing* the self, of *gaining wisdom* by virtue of understanding, feeling the influence of, and being with the Radiant Forces in your life.

This knowledge and wisdom are often referred to as self-realization in spiritual and mystical writings. The move to Level 3 is where the Attractions come in. In a sense, we are attracted to our own self-realization.

A RECAP OF THREE LEVELS OF ATTRACTION

Level 1: We feel a desire, need, or compulsion toward some goal or objective. In following that desire, life unfolds before us.

Level 2: We recognize that we are attracted to a *state of being* that is more inside us than outside in the imagined future of the thing we wish to obtain. We are aware of the pull toward this state of being and the process of moving toward it.

Level 3: We recognize that our Attraction is an attraction toward the Radiant Forces at a deeper soulful level.* In our movement with the Radiant Forces, we both enfold information and unfold ourselves and our life.

You start to understand that your life story—as a whole unfolding—has always resulted from your attraction to something greater than you currently know. When you have this understanding, you tap into your purpose, calling, cause, legacy, or destiny.

The objective of *QfP Book 3* is to help you articulate a richer sense of the Attractions and how they show up in your personal experience of life.

✦ Where are you in the unfolding story of your life?

✦ What new information is being enfolded into your story that gives you a sense of where you might be headed?

✦ What is unfolding in your life that has nothing to do with clock-time?

✦ What Treasures, soulful stirrings, and aspirations are being enfolded as you journey through your day, week, or month?

✦ From another perspective, what have you been sent here to do or, better, to be?

*Level 3 Attraction—knowing the self, gaining wisdom, moving toward something greater—supports tempognosis. This process is defined in the QfP primer, *The Connoisseur of Time,* as having knowledge (gnosis) of time (tempo) for nurturing the journey of the soul in this life.

Contemplation (QfP 3-1): Intuition, Mystery, and You

This contemplation has two parts. First, rate yourself on the survey statements below. Second, after reviewing your answers, reflect on the questions below and consider journaling about them or sharing in a discussion group.

	Not at All True	A Little True	Somewhat True	True	Very True
1. I am an intuitive person.	☐	☐	☐	☐	☐
2. I see life as a mystery.	☐	☐	☐	☐	☐
3. My life is unfolding in ways that make me curious.	☐	☐	☐	☐	☐
4. Forces are at work to bring me along in my life journey.	☐	☐	☐	☐	☐
5. Events in my life are unfolding in ways that reveal some meaning or purpose.	☐	☐	☐	☐	☐
6. My day-to-day life is more than mechanical routines.	☐	☐	☐	☐	☐
7. Events in my life that were painful or challenging also had a purpose.	☐	☐	☐	☐	☐
8. I have felt that my life is moving along according to some predestined plan.	☐	☐	☐	☐	☐
9. My time in this life depends on what I make of it.	☐	☐	☐	☐	☐
10. I have felt a mysterious and spontaneous quickening, stirring, or inspiration which led me to see the world in a new way.	☐	☐	☐	☐	☐

	Not at All True	A Little True	Somewhat True	True	Very True
11. I have felt too tied to the calendar or schedule, trying to fit everything in, and wish I could just let it all go.	☐	☐	☐	☐	☐

QUESTIONS

1. Reflect on the statements above. Which one of the items "speaks" to you the most? Which one made you think about some deeper aspect of your sense of self? Explain why it did.

2. What is happening in your life that is attracting you to something different, to the next page, a new vista, a reveal, a newness? Note that this can be something very subtle, small, and apparently insignificant.

3. Based on your answers to the above, how can you perceive that time—your experience of time in your life—is more than just mechanical clock-time? Explain.

4. What is it *within you* that has this perception?

5. What is attracting you to your purpose, cause, calling, legacy, or destiny? Consider both "external" factors—people, places, cultural factors, areas of study, religious or spiritual beliefs—and "internal" factors—your talents, strengths, dreams, intuitions, memories, and fantasies.

6. (With a group discussion) Ask each person to share which of the statements was the most engaging or provocative and explain why. Also, which item was the most confusing or difficult to answer and explain why.

CHAPTER 2

Finding Your Bearings

An Ode to Attractions

Thieves call out to you at night:
 This is not your story
 You are finding your way

Priests beckon you into the temple:
 This is your story
 The way is finding you

Some crazed hobo:
 Let's get away from them
 Let's get lost in the woods

This wizard cult will find us
A motley and careless bunch
Sway and juke around an untamed fire:
 sensuous dancers, calculating warriors,
 deceiving simpletons, and those who
 give counsel

  They all offer the same bribe:
   step outside
   your
   shivering
   evanescent
   self

       ~J.B.

Your personality, that which makes you unique, shapes the outward story of this happening life. Your personality can also reveal the inner workings of your essential nature. You can build self-awareness of your personality as you orient to the precious time you have remaining in this life. Such awareness—your observing self—allows you to tap into the essence that is enfolded within your personality. Because of your personality, you may have a tendency to witness some Treasures more than others, see the workings of certain spiritual principles, and benefit from certain spiritual practices.

In the journey of life, the state in which we often find ourselves is due to the paths we have chosen, those that destiny has chosen for us, or those somewhere in between. Some spiritual teachers call this *effort and grace*; our soul flies on two wings: one effort, the other grace. Our flight path is greatly influenced by our personality traits, attitudes, motives, predilections, and addictions. Also, these traits and predilections are influenced by deeper and soulful aspects of our being.

I have never met anyone who did not have some soulful aspect of their being shining through their current state. We all are carrying a deeper imprint. It is only because we get too focused or "caught up" in our situation that we fail to see the deeper pattern of this happening life: the trails we leave behind and the arcs we create on our flight. Again, we take ourselves too seriously instead of just witnessing life unfold.

Your ego, or limited sense of personality as a fixed trait, is both (a) the most significant barrier to seeing the forces at work in your life and, paradoxically, (b) a path toward seeing those forces. Have you ever had any of these beliefs: "I am who I am" or "This is the way I do things" or "My way is the best way"? Such beliefs can prevent you from seeing the weave, the underlying threads, the preciousness. The ego is not able to pierce the veil because the veil is the ego.

Much, but not all, of modern psychology has fixated on a fairly structured or "type" view of personality. There are dozens of personality surveys on strengths, styles, types, archetypes. The problem is that they tend to reinforce the illusion that we are fixed beings, that we may not be as subject to change as we might like. Instead, remember that you are on a journey. You are going somewhere. You are attracted to the Treasure that is seeking you.

BOX 2.1: TOWARD A DYNAMIC VIEW OF SELF

Readers interested in a scientific basis for a more dynamic and non-"type" view of the self may also be interested in research on two fields of study: self-construal and construal-level theory. Before I explain these ideas, I ask that you first review each of these statements and select one that you like the best.

1. I do my own thing regardless of what others think.

2. It is important for me to maintain harmony in my group.

3. I am aware of a connection between myself and all living things.

Self-construal generally refers to the ways we view our self (construe our self-concept). We continually form an image or atlas of our self in reference to our culture, to others, relationships, social groups, and also to time. *Construal-level* theory states that people have direct experience only of the here and now. Accordingly, we create mental simulations or abstract ideas to represent objects and events that we cannot directly access through our senses; scientists call these simulations *construals*. These objects and events also take place further into the future; scientists call this *temporal distance*.

Our view of our self depends upon time (The Radiant Forces). Studies suggest that how we perceive or project time is based on how we construe our self-concept and vice versa; our relationship to our self is based on our assumptions and beliefs about time. For example, having a more individualistic and independent view of the self as separate from others (see statement 1 above) results in seeing events taking longer (time expansion). This is because of the sense of agency or compulsion to act borne from Time Shaping. In contrast, having a more collective or interdependent view of oneself as connected to others (see statement 2 above) correlates with suspended action. We see events as taking less time. Here, we attune more to Nurturing Conditions—letting things unfold.

Other studies suggest that self-construal relates to functions of Chaos: ambiguity, anxiety, perceived threats, uncontrollability, or being interrupted. Seeing the world in a more holistic and less analytic manner (seeing the big picture rather than focusing on details) relates to decreased anxiety. Those with interdependent self-construal tend to have this more holistic cognition, potentially as a way to reduce the threat of isolation that may come about through chaotic events. When we excessively focus on a task, an interruption leads to negative emotions. Those with independent self-construal are more prone to this reactivity because they compress time. Tendencies toward Form—rumination, repetitive thinking, getting stuck in a negative loop—also impact us. Those who ruminate are more likely to perceive certain events as a threat.

A metapersonal view. Our sense of self develops and emerges over time as we relate to and contend with different forces. Studies suggest that we each can also have a holistic or metapersonal view of our self. This way of construing our self, one that considers and works with all the forces, may be the best for our well-being. Specifically, a new approach proposes "metapersonal self-construal" as different from independent and interdependent self-construal. Again, consider these three statements:

1. I do my own thing, regardless of what others think.

2. It is important for me to maintain harmony in my group.

3. I am aware of a connection between myself and all living things.

In item 1 (independent), we construe our self as existing *in time as a single entity* and beyond the influence of others. In item 2 (interdependent), we construe our self as existing within a *group over time.* In item 3 (metapersonal), we construe our self as existing *within time itself, and even outside of time,* and with all things over time.

Research suggests that each of these forms of self-construal has benefits when used in a thoughtful and mindful manner and that we can become flexible. We can pivot from one type of construal to another rather than stay rigid in our self-construal. Importantly, researchers' self-assessments of the metapersonal mode are similar to other questionnaires described in *QfP Book 2: self-transcendence, spiritual health,* and *spiritual well-being.* As we proceed on our quest, we may loosen the ego and take the "person" out of personality. In our attraction to "meta," the self becomes a spiritual self.

If everything happens because of the operation of the four Radiant Forces, then everything also happens as a result of our personality or how we construe our self in and over time. Our personality exists in between our current state of life and the more eternal or enduring essence of our being. In *QfP Book 2: The Soulful Capacities*, we explore this essence in more depth. Later in this chapter, I offer you a tool to help you get your bearings toward the four Radiant Forces. The purpose of the Quest for Presence Inventory™ (QFPI™) is to help you notice your preferences and attractions and return to a center, a place of observing the journey.

Noticing Your Preference for How You Spend or Relate to Time

Some of the other books in the Q*f*P collection ask whether you *prefer* Form, Time Shaping, Nurturing Conditions, or Chaos. Another way to frame this question is to ask whether you are "attracted" to one of these more than another. Perhaps you have an Attraction to some of the forces more than the others. Look at the current state of your life.

1. Is your life made up of fairly regular routines and schedules so that if there are problems, things are fairly organized, and you are able to easily return to a regular and steady lifestyle?

2. Do you spend a good deal of time moving from one activity to another? Do you tend to stay busy pursuing goals and always have lots to do?

3. Is the majority of your time spent cultivating interests, exploring how you can serve, working with and through your intuition, or just taking an open attitude toward allowing things to happen?

4. Are things often "up in the air?" Do you think life is chaotic, uncertain, unplanned?

Notice How Your Attraction to a State Changes

Reflect for a moment on whether your answers to the questions above are true only for right now or whether they are more permanent. Is the state of your happening life *always* organized, *always* busy, *always* cultivating, or *always* chaotic? It is possible that it is or that it is not. Either way, it is very rare that we spend our time only in one state.

And yet, we do have an overall Attraction at certain points or stages in life. That is, our soul is called or pulled in a general direction throughout the course of our happening life. It is this underlying Attraction to one state over another that begins to reveal our personality to us. Some of us tend to move around during important transition points, such as after major challenges, periods of initiation, or entering into or leaving a relationship or career. It is possible to transition from one Attraction to another. Yet many of us tend to hover around a particular area or come back to it again and again.

Consider Your Attraction as a Call from Your Soul

Imagine that our map is laid out on a two-dimensional grid, like the one shown on page 37. Notice that the lines on this grid suggest a weave or a combination of forces at work, setting up somewhat of a "force field." Imagine this as a continuously changing field of waves moving in different directions. This happening life is going on right now in this force field. You are constantly moving into and out of different states within this field.

In other words, you are always *attracted* to a state of being. A key principle in your Quest for Presence is that your state of being will, over the course of your life, always move in the direction of bringing out your essence or deeper nature.

That last statement is worth repeating. Again:

Your state of being will, over the course of your life, always move in the direction of bringing out your essence or deeper nature.

Your Attraction is a powerful driving force within the force field, a force that gives birth to your experience of the force field. In a special way, your Attraction creates the entire field, the entire totality of the map, the precious weave.

Unattractive States

There will be times in your life when it will look like, feel, or seem as though you are attracted to pain, failure, ugliness, negativity, or any undesirable state—even the desire to do harm. The part of you that experiences unattractive states reflects those aspects of your personality that are undergoing some type of transformation. And that transformation is often about some revelation of your essence. You may be in a rut, lost, empty, or uncertain. But these states are only temporary. Consider how these experiences reflect the operations of the four Radiant Forces.

✦ Have you ever felt that your life is stuck in the same rut, or you cannot seem to shake free of some pattern, addiction, or unproductive routine? (Reflect on how this inertia, a sense of being held down by gravity, may be the work of Form.)

✦ Have you ever felt that life is just a set of meaningless activities, of staying busy, or of just going from one activity or situation to another; go, go, go? (Reflect on how this overactive state, a sense of having to always prepare for action, may be the work of Time Shaping.)

✦ Have you ever felt that you lose yourself, lose your way, or have given yourself over to something or someone? Have there been times when you just have to let go and trust even though you really don't want to? (Reflect on how these experiences, of being forced to see the bigger picture, may be the work of Nurturing Conditions.)

✦ Have you ever felt your life is in shambles, broken, completely out of control, without any hope or sense of footing? (Reflect on how this may be the work of Chaos.)

The upcoming survey exercise (QFPI™) is designed to help you get your bearings in and through these kinds of experiences; to help you gain insight into the big picture and how you—your personality—may be attracted to certain states. Should you ever feel that you linger in one state more than another, reflect on the image shown. This image, the matrix of attractions, is a reflection of the precious weave of life forces that are enfolded within your personality.

A Practice for the Observing Self

In my previous book, *Raw Coping Power,* I described the *Inner Guardian* as a metaphor for mental and emotional processes that help us calmly observe events and protect us from the negative effects of stress. The observing self is the same thing as this inner guardian. You can begin to develop this observer by reviewing the above factors and taking the Quest for Presence Inventory™. Notice what you prefer, how your attraction to states changes, and how you are moving in the direction of your essence: these are efforts made by the observing self.

> *No matter what takes place, no matter what we experience, nothing is as central as the self that observes …The most important fact about the observing self is that it is incapable of being objectified … it is not part of the objective world. Thus, everyday consciousness contains a transcendent element that we seldom notice because that element is the very ground of our experience (Deikman, 1982).*

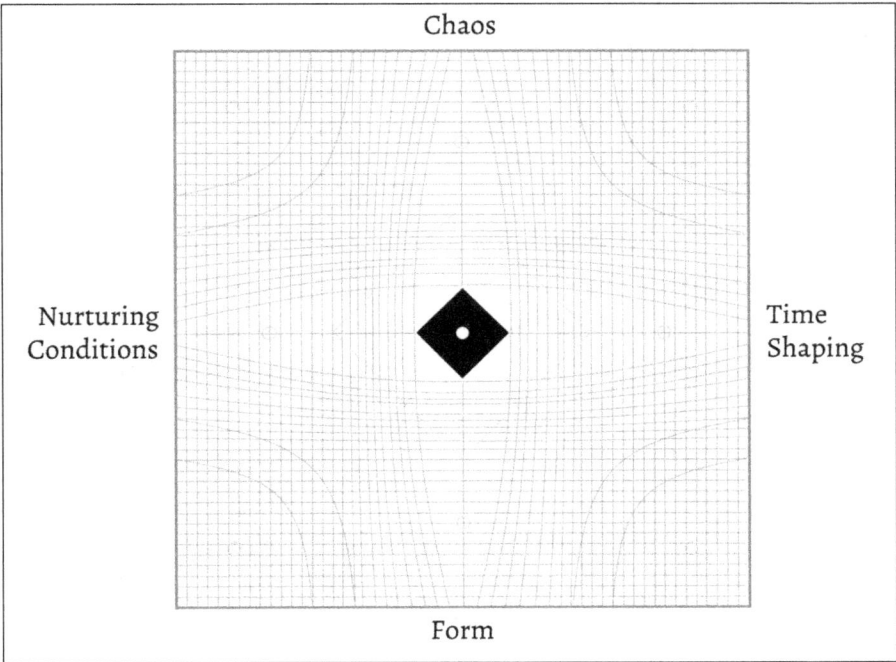

The Quest for Presence Inventory™

The following questionnaire is not intended in any way to categorize your style or type. Its purpose is not to "peg" you as being one certain way. Instead, it is an imperfect method, a pointer, an estimate of a reality. As mentioned above, questionnaires in modern psychology—something called the *science of* psychometrics—distorts our truest nature by overemphasizing a quantitative view of ourselves, our personality. You are not a number. No part of you can ever be reduced to a number. To help you grasp this idea, take your time to read the following lines.

I am a force
Within a set of radiant forces
That are shaping a force
That is right now shaping me

It is for this reason that I do not suggest taking this survey until after you have read the preceding chapter. Please also review the following "commitment" statements before taking the survey. Remember, we are talking about your life that is happening right now, and the fact that right now, something is working to bring out your essence. Something is "afoot" that is fulfilling your attraction to your fullest expression or destiny. You are on the threshold of being able to walk into your life in a new way.

As you read each of the statements, consider how you can align with or own them as written. Really chew on each statement, turn it over in your mind as you think about it.

Standard questionnaires ask you to rate how much you agree (for example, on a 5-point scale from "Strongly Disagree" to "Strongly Agree"). The following statements pertain more to how you *own* your experience of the discovery process. Whether you can or cannot *agree* with the statements is not relevant. Whether you can *align* with them to a lesser or greater degree is not relevant. What is relevant is *the process* that awakens within you as you consider them.

Use the following Commitment Statements as an initiation. The journey has begun. From this point forward you are, in a way, on your own. Specifically, you are now living *within* the question ("quest"-ion): *How is my life now aligning with the four cosmic Radiant Forces?*

Attraction Matrix Commitment Statements

I am committed to

1. *opening* to how my life is a process of being attracted to my essence or essential nature;

2. *seeing* my attraction to different forces working right now to bring out my true *potential*;

3. *centering* myself in the deep emergence of organic time whenever I feel caught up in clock-time;

4. *dancing* and *crafting* with the deeper rhythms of time that unfold in my life right now;

5. *discerning* and *letting go* of the need for clock-time in my life;

6. *being open* to the possibility, the potential, or the auspiciousness of becoming someone wholly different from the person I am now;

7. *cultivating* Soulful Capacities that will enrich my life, my full presence on this planet;

8. *getting my bearings* or coordinates from day to each enlightening day;

9. *finding balance;* whenever I feel the opposition of forces, I stretch fully into them.

I (write your name) _____, am owner of the above Commitment Statements and see they will facilitate the evolution of my consciousness as a human being.

THE QUEST FOR PRESENCE INVENTORY™
(QFPI™ ATTRACTION SCALE)

Following are a series of pairs of statements. Examining one pair at a time, decide which statement you agree with or prefer more. For Pair 1, do you agree more with (X) or (Y)?

Indicate the degree to which you prefer (X) or (Y) by circling the number from 1 to 6. If you agree with (X) and not with (Y), then you would select number "1." If you agree somewhere "in between" (X) or (Y), you would select a number from "2" to "5." If you agree with (Y) and not with (X), then you would circle "6."

For example, if you felt only a slight preference for (X) you might mark like this:

X Statement		O			Y Statement

If you felt a strong, but not complete preference for (Y) you might mark like this:

X Statement				O		Y Statement

Note that the scoring sequence, from "1" to "6" or "6" to "1" differs from item to item.

	X Statement							Y Statement	
1.	Many factors lead to the shape of future events, including my past and present actions.	1	2	3	4	5	6	I can shape future events by taking thoughtful actions now.	A
2.	I enjoy work that has order and procedures.	6	5	4	3	2	1	I enjoy work that involves risks and surprises.	B
3.	Obstacles to getting what I want are challenges I enjoy.	6	5	4	3	2	1	Both obstacles and helpful factors influence my course of action.	A

	X Statement							Y Statement	
4.	I prefer to take each day as it comes because I work best when I can be spontaneous.	1	2	3	4	5	6	I prefer working with schedules and calendars to organize time in my life.	B
5.	I would enjoy gardening because I get to work with the soil, sunlight, and nutrients to create optimal conditions for growth.	1	2	3	4	5	6	I would enjoy gardening because planting seeds and working the soil can eventually yield an abundant harvest.	A
6.	I work best when projects have clear objectives and when the structure and activities are planned out.	6	5	4	3	2	1	I work best when I can immerse myself in a creative project and where there is less concern about outcomes.	B
7.	Each individual has the chance to create the positive outcomes they wish to see in the world.	6	5	4	3	2	1	Given the right conditions, a small group of inspired people can bring about positive change for others.	A
8.	What matters most in life is the people we meet and our ability to help each other along the way.	1	2	3	4	5	6	What matters most in life is leaving a legacy of useful achievements or accomplishments.	A
9.	I prefer to play and experiment with new ideas and explore the unknown.	1	2	3	4	5	6	I prefer to work with known methods and established guidelines.	B
10.	To stay healthy, I prefer to follow a regular schedule of exercise and healthy eating.	6	5	4	3	2	1	To stay healthy, I prefer doing activities I enjoy or that create a sense of flow and excitement.	B

Continue to the next page before scoring

A score total ☐   B score total ☐

	X Statement							Y Statement	
11.	I work with the nuances and changes in situations so I can influence outcomes that work best.	1	2	3	4	5	6	I schedule events to achieve certain and often specific outcomes.	A
12.	I don't mind being interrupted or interrupting others in a deep conversation.	1	2	3	4	5	6	I prefer taking turns in conversation so that each person has a chance to speak.	B
13.	Once I see that a course of action is required, I feel it is urgent to get it done.	6	5	4	3	2	1	I typically wait for things to fall into place before taking action.	A
14.	To stay healthy, I take charge of my situation and follow a plan for a healthy lifestyle.	6	5	4	3	2	1	To stay healthy, I take a relaxed approach and do things in moderation.	A
15.	My actions follow the philosophy of embracing the ups and downs of life: "Whatever will be will be."	1	2	3	4	5	6	My actions follow the philosophy of order and preparation: "It is best to line your ducks up in a row."	B
16.	Time is a bridge that connects the past to the future.	1	2	3	4	5	6	Time is a ladder reaching into the future or a train moving to the future.	A
17.	Each event in my life leads to the next in a clear and orderly way.	6	5	4	3	2	1	My life is filled with mystery and interesting twists and turns.	B
18.	Success depends on many factors, our own personal growth, and the "right time."	1	2	3	4	5	6	Success depends on our own actions and "seizing the moment."	A

	X Statement							Y Statement	
19.	What matters most is enjoying what one has today.	1	2	3	4	5	6	What matters most is stability and security.	B
20.	Time is a reality; past, present, and future are each important.	6	5	4	3	2	1	Time is an illusion; all that exists is the current moment.	B

A score total ☐   B score total ☐

HOW TO SCORE THE QFPI™

PART 1. Total your ratings for all previous 20 items in the following way. You will get two scores (each should range between 10 and 60). One total score for all ten "A" items and one total score for all ten "B" items. You can easily see which item is either "A" or "B" by looking at the far-right column. The item numbers for each statement are also shown below.

A) Add up your ratings for items 1,3,5,7,8,11,13,14,16,18

→ Score _____

B) Add up your ratings for items 2,4,6,9,10,12,15,17,19,20

→ Score _____

PART 2. For the second part, you will take your two scores and plot them as coordinates on the grid below. There are three steps to this part.

Step 1. For your A score, mark an X on the top horizontal axis (left ←→ right) below. That is, look at the top of the grid with the numbers ranging from "10" on the left to "60" on the right. Make a mark on your score along the top.

Step 2. For your B score, mark an X on the side vertical axis (up ↑↓ down) below. That is, look at the left of the grid with scores ranging from "10" at the top to "60" at the bottom. Make a mark on your score on the left-hand side of the grid.

Step 3. Find the intersection point on the grid where your two points meet. This is your **QFPI™ Attraction** score. On the next pages, you will learn more about what this score means.

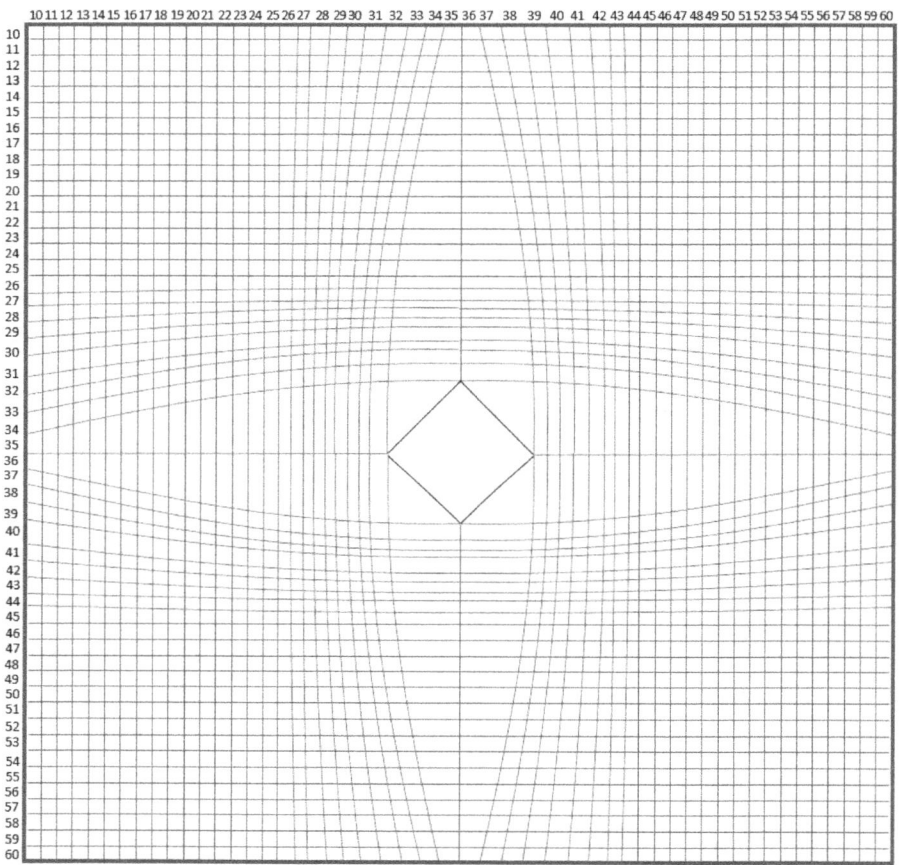

The graph on page 46 provides an example of how this would look based on my own scores. My A score was a 26 (horizontal mark on top). My B score was a 27 (vertical score on the left). I plotted the coordinates where the two scores meet on the grid. This is shown by an open circle on the grid. This circle is closest to the Crafting quadrant. It is also in between Potentiating, Opening, and Synthesizing. Below, in the descriptions of these different attractions, I will review Crafting but also will want to know about these other Attractions.

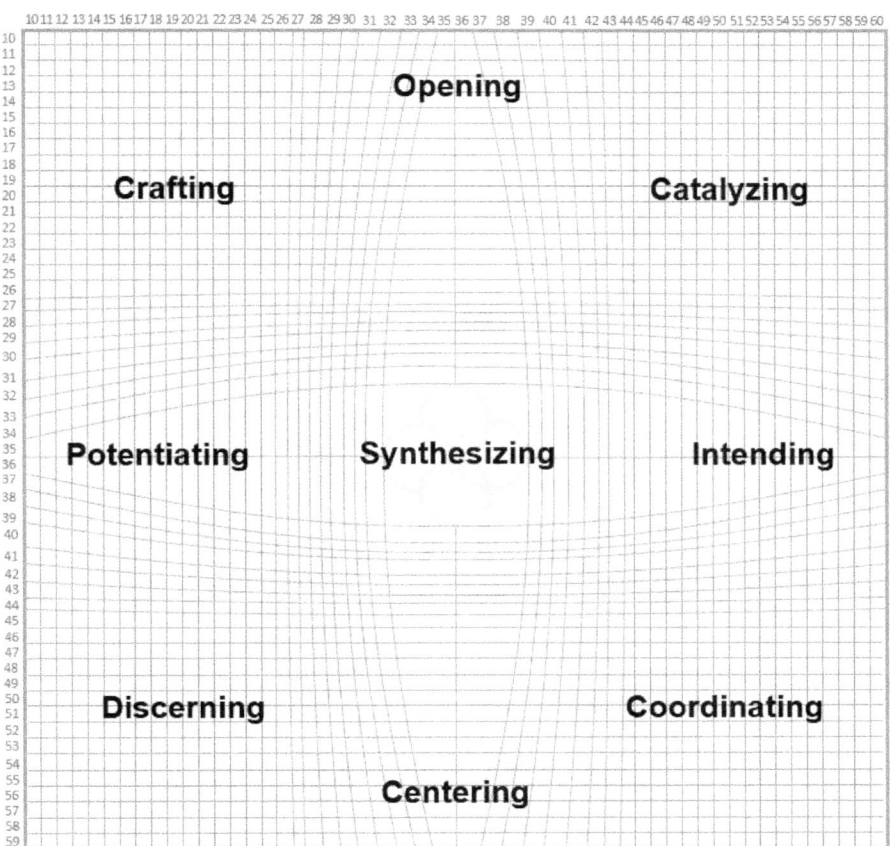

Opening

Crafting

Catalyzing

Potentiating

Synthesizing

Intending

Discerning

Coordinating

Centering

In looking at the two scores and how they coincide on the chart, it is helpful to draw some contrasts. This is to help you understand how to use the chart and also to understand how your Attraction is not a fixed or static quality. Let's say my score was shown as the diamond or the square on the grid. The diamond is more toward the extreme corner of the Crafting quadrant. This suggests that Crafting is a much stronger Attraction than the others. Hence, I may want to pay more attention to what is happening in my life that draws me more strongly to Crafting. In the next chapter, when reading about Crafting, I will want to pay even closer attention to this attraction.

For further comparison, let's say my scores are conveyed by the square, located right between Potentiating and Synthesizing. This suggests that both of these might have an equal Attraction for me. Something is happening in my life that is drawing me toward working with both of these energies or attractions. When I consult the descriptions below, I would want to look at both Potentiating and Synthesizing.

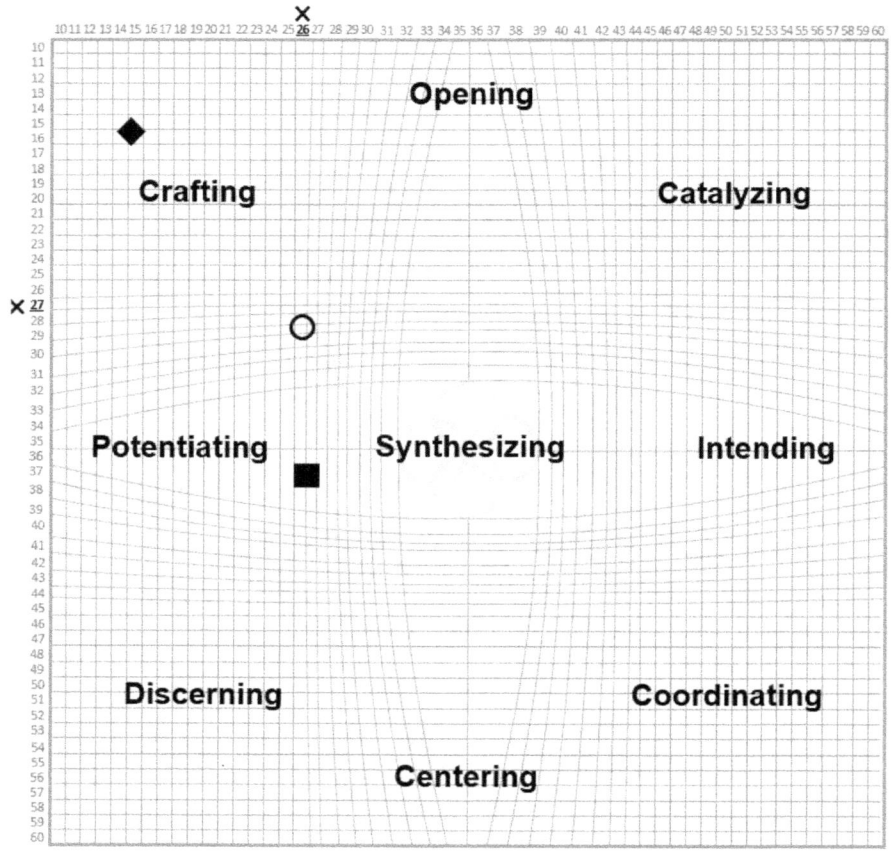

Now, imagine that you take the QFPI™ several times over the course of weeks or months. It is possible (and even likely) that your scores will vary or fluctuate over time. This can mean any number of things—for example, changes in mood or your interpretation of a word while you were taking the questionnaire. It can also mean actual fluctuations in your Attraction. Indeed, the circle, square, and diamond represent different times in my own life when I have taken QFPI™. The single snapshot in time when we answer the questions does not fully represent the dynamic and changing nature of our Attraction. The Radiant Forces are always dancing into our happening life, and we—because of the growth in our awareness of essence—blur along with these dynamics. Hence, a more accurate picture of our Attraction is more like a cloud or blur with varying degrees of fuzziness and light.

The image below conveys this blur. It suggests that my Attraction is to all three areas: Crafting, Potentiating, and Synthesizing. In the story, narrative, or course of my own fulfillment, my essence is drawn to learning and discovery in this space more often than in other spaces represented in the entire grid.

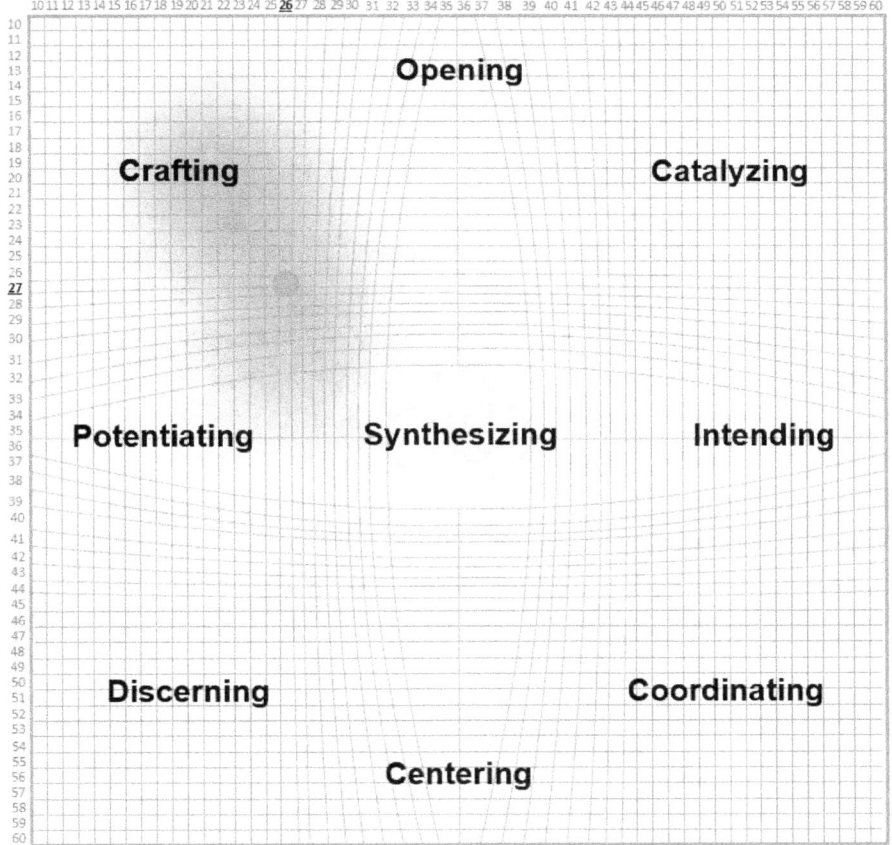

Interpreting the Quest for Presence Inventory™ (QFPI™)

It is important to keep these different ideas or tendencies in mind as you explore the meaning of your score and avoid feeling that you have to "pin down" your Attraction with a single score. Nine feedback forms with associated interpretations of the QFPI™ Attractions are provided in the next chapter. In some cases, the position of a score will be clearly in a particular quadrant or right next to the periphery of the entire square. This is shown in the example of the diamond above. This case illustrates what I call a "singular and primary" Attraction, and it may suggest that one focus only on the feedback form for that Attraction. In other cases, the position of a score may fall in between two areas and may lean toward one or another Attraction. In the example of the square above, this would suggest a primary tendency toward Synthesizing (also called Integrating) (as it is closer) and a secondary tendency toward Potentiating or Nurturing. In this case, you would have primary and secondary Attractions, and you would examine both feedback forms.

Still, in other cases, your score may be ambiguous, as might be the case with the open circle above. While the tendency is within the Crafting quadrant, the position suggests equal leanings toward both Synthesizing and Potentiating. Here, you would look at all three feedback forms to self-assess: (a) which fits best, (b) whether you are in transition from one to another Attraction, or (c) all Attractions have something to contribute to your self-understanding. Again, it is for you to discern what your Attraction is. Use this as a tool for that purpose. By the way, many of us are often in transition, and it is helpful to be accepting and present to the transition.

Contemplation (Q*f*P 3-2):
Stop Reading, and Go with Your Gut

This contemplation works only if you stop here before moving forward to read the next chapter. After all, the purpose of a contemplation is that one takes a pause to reflect.

Key Questions: What did you notice as you read the commitments and then made your ratings? What phrases or words stood out or resonated with you? What sense do you have of what is happening? What do your heart, gut, and intuition tell you?

Imagine that this is all the information you need. You don't need to read the next chapter. Use your intuition. **Give your own intuitive interpretation to your score on the grid.**

CHAPTER 3

The Nine Attractions

An Ode to You

You think you can take your time;
But, in the end, time will take you.

They say: It's pretty cut-and-dried.

You think you know there is
a time for everything;
But, in the end, time is what you make of it.

They say: Get with the program.

You think time is on your side;
But, in the end, time just slips away.

They say: All things must pass.

You think that time forgives all sin;
But, in the end, time just runs out.

They say: The devil always gets his due.

What do they really know?
All these thoughtless platitudes.

Have they really taken the time to
sit there, drink some tea,
and get to know you?
The real you.

And that miracle gift,
that angel dancing in your chest?

With its own rhythm and smile,
watching the many-sided swirl,
the great undoing with all
that glitter
and wrapping paper.

~J.B.

On the following pages, you will find descriptions (feedback forms) for each of the nine personality energies or Attractions. Beware of any tendency to place too much emphasis on your QFPI™ score. Instead, I encourage you to read through all the descriptions and notice which ones resonate most with you. Your ability to accurately identify your Attraction (at this time) may depend upon your Soulful Capacity "level" (as assessed in *QfP Book 2: The Soulful Capacities*).

Each of the nine Attraction feedback forms contains the following elements. Please note that the feedback forms emphasize how the Attractions may show up and be worked with in your career or occupational setting. At the same time, the Attraction manifests in similar ways within relationships.

Interpreting the Personality

+ **Signifier and Synonyms.** The image of a person in dynamic poses is shown at the beginning of each Attraction to signify the energy and general posture the Attraction takes in its dynamic state of attraction to the Radiant Forces. This image is only a suggested pictorial representation to help make the dynamic concept of Attraction more concrete. There are many other ways to visualize the Attraction (or the combinations of them). We use a single word to convey an Attraction, and there are other alternate words or synonyms that may resonate more with you. These synonyms are essential to review as they speak to the nuances in and dynamic nature of the meaning of each Attraction. Use whatever term or phrase you feel best captures your own sense of the Attraction. What word speaks most directly to your current unfolding?

✦ **Key Quote.** Many quotes capture the spirit of each Attraction. I selected those that offer accessible illustrations. Again, I invite you to find others that may resonate more personally.

✦ **Primary Attraction and Description.** These are brief descriptions of the Attractions, especially with a focus on their orientation toward time. Reading these in conjunction with the embodiments gives a full sense of the Attraction.

✦ **Embodiments in Relationships.** The same process occurs in relationships. You may find yourself in an intimate relationship or partnership, preferring to do something entirely different from your partner. Partner preferences do not always coincide. I recommend that you share your Attraction preferences with your partner and find ways that you complement each other. The best thing about this exercise is that you may discover how your partner can give you better access to certain Treasures and vice versa.

✦ **Embodiments in Career, Professions.** Sometimes, but not always, because of your certain Attractions, you can end up working in (or have a desire to work in) a particular profession. It also happens that your chosen profession may become adapted or accustomed to the Attraction. Specifically, other people in your life and career may think that your "work face" is who you are. But in truth, you may be secretly working behind the scenes to give full expression to your Attraction. For example, I have worked with people in project-management positions that would seem (on the surface) to be the domain of an Organizer. However, the way they did their job—managed projects—was to facilitate the team working better together (see **Attraction in Work Style**, below). Hence, their main Attraction was Potentiating. I recommend sharing your Attraction (your QFPI™ score) with your work colleagues along with how you think your "true" self often shows up at work. Be open to feedback about how you are seen.*

✦ **Attraction in Work Style.** As explained in the section above, sometimes Attractions can manifest in a tendency to work in certain types of jobs or careers. More specifically, the Attraction can result in a particular style of work and manner in which you interact with others at work. It is important to remember that this is related to—but different from—your profession. It has more to do with how you *fit* into the workflow and your surrounding team and your general orientation to any product or service within your work.

✦ **Cautions in Working with Others.** If you agree that your Attraction (your QFPI™ score) reflects your reality, then it may help to be aware of how your approach may be a challenge to others. If we have not developed our Soulful Capacity, we may be less aware of how our actions influence or have an impact on those around us.

✦ **The Challenge (Stuck in this Space).** It is possible that your Attraction is also a stumbling block or obstacle to your experience of this happening life, especially in the field of work or career. In many ways, knowing your inherent challenge can be the best barometer of your Attraction. Joseph Campbell's quote *"Where you stumble, there lies your treasure"* applies here. I recommend reading through the **Challenge** sections for all the Attractions. The ones that irritate you most or give you a sense that something is off (a "glitch") may signal your Attraction.

---

* Part 2 of this book (especially Chapters 5 and 6) give some examples of how the Attractions manifest at work. Please also consult the Appendix for a brief case study where we used the QFPI™ with a team of colleagues.

+ **Corrections.** These are suggestions for steps you can take to correct your approach based on the cautions listed above. Overall, the best corrections lie in cultivating the Soulful Capacities and exploring how these capacities can help you when you're faced with the challenges or the different preferences of others. At the same time, many corrections can come from welcoming the approach and Attractions of others who are not like you. I recommend reading through all nine Attraction profiles, with special attention paid to the **Corrections** sections of each.

+ **Affirmations.** I offer a selection of brief sayings or positive aphorisms for each Attraction. As with the key quotes, you can use many different turns of phrase to stay centered on your quest for presence. The best affirmations are those you create yourself and have a present tense, positive, and self-coherent feel to them. You know a good affirmation if it inspires you.

+ **Treasures.** Treasures are those moments of clarity that bring us beyond ourselves and the mundane sense of clock-time. Each Attraction inclines toward certain Treasures more than others. Therefore, another way to discern your Attraction is to notice if certain Treasures occur more often or keep showing up in your life. The brief description in this segment of the Attraction feedback form can point you to explore ways that your personality overlaps with—and can benefit from—these principles, values, and practices.

OPENING

"Dance, when you're broken open. Dance, if you've torn the bandage off. Dance in the middle of the fighting. Dance in your blood. Dance when you're perfectly free."

~JALĀL AD-DĪN MOHAMMAD RŪMĪ, KNOWN AS RUMI, PERSIAN POET, ISLAMIC SCHOLAR (1207–1273)

Synonyms: breaking open, broadening, creating anew, disappearing, discontinuing, escaping, expanding, exploring, mutating, radicalizing, releasing, revolutionizing, stumbling, transcending, transforming, unclothing, unknowing, unraveling, wobbling (also "Innovating")

Primary Attraction: Willingness to try something new and innovate from a fresh perspective; able to relax preconceptions and play with situations from a new angle. The passion for creating, creative initiatives, starting new projects, or creating something out of nothing can provide the fuel and energy needed for a long-term engagement, relationship, journey, or project.

Description: When innovating, we view and embrace time in all its chaotic qualities. The tendency here is to fully immerse yourself and your projects in the creative process and view this process as an end in itself rather than as a means to achieve something, meet some goal, or design or deliver a specific product. Accordingly, there is a tendency to relax clock-time constraints and ignore mainstay approaches to time management (schedules, calendars, to-do lists, and planners).

Time management is relevant only insofar as it supports the creative process. The process absorbs you fully, and the content of life takes care of itself.

Embodiments in Relationships: You prefer to try new places and enjoy experimenting with different ideas in being with another. Prone to spontaneity. Prefer exploring and novelty over stability and sameness.

Embodiments in Career, Professions: Working in creative or expressive arts; free-thinking; experimenter; explorer; inventor; entrepreneur. As a leader, you may be prone to say, "Let's get away, turn off all the clocks, and brainstorm and come up with something that no one has thought of yet."

Attraction in Work Style: The strongest attraction is for design aspects of work and the enjoyment of pulling together and using materials for innovating a new type of approach. On a team, this manifests as the person who thinks outside the box and could design something that is both disruptive and effective. This is more likely when times or workplace norms have changed, and there is little concern or resistance to those changes.

Cautions in Working/Relating with Others: Others may feel that you are not grounded in reality or that your creative ideas will take too long to implement. They may also fail to understand how they can put your ideas into operation within a reasonable time frame.

The Challenge (Stuck in this Space): The tendency to see creativity or design as the only worthwhile endeavor, and, as a result, the innovation may not have the basis that is required for working in the real world. Others may complain: "Great idea, but it has no legs—we'll never get this done" or "You are way ahead of your time" or "People will think that is ... weird or too 'out there'"!

Corrections: Seeking out those attracted to organizing and engineering. Grounding your ideas in a strategic plan with clear, actionable steps that lead to clearly defined objectives. Avoiding becoming overwhelmed with scheduling details so you don't lose your creative momentum.

Affirmations: I effectively turn my creative impulse into actionable steps, and this results in a successful and health-giving project. The journey is well worth the effort. I am grounded in the meaning of life and adore those I live and work with.

Treasures: Abide in Awe (reverence, wonder) and Spontaneity (play, playfulness), and look for randomness.

CATALYZING

"The greater the difficulty, the more glory in surmounting it."
~EPICTETUS, GREEK PHILOSOPHER (55–135 AD)

"If you obey all the rules, you'll miss all the fun."
~KATHARINE HEPBURN, AMERICAN ACTRESS (1907–2003)

Synonyms: altering, bringing (positive) audacity, breaking up (the old), bringing out (the truth), challenging, championing, confronting, contesting, contradicting, converting, debating, dismantling, encountering (the unknown), epitomizing, igniting, initiating, inspiring (others to take up the challenge), protesting, questioning, repatterning

Primary Attraction: Willingness to stand up and act against processes and operations that are status quo, inhibiting growth, or simply no longer work. There is a drive to anticipate, find, and address obstacles and barriers, and uncover factors, often for implementing any new exploration, process, strategy, or program. Sometimes this drive is what is needed to make a relationship, process, or program work when other approaches have failed. There is an associated willingness to take on unsuspected and surprising challenges that others might avoid.

Description: Viewing time in terms of occasions or incidents (present or future) that must be addressed to reach a goal or outcome (often immediate or emergent). The tendency here is to view obstacles as robust opportunities to develop yourself, others, clients, or your workplace (the obstacle is the way). Accordingly, time has both a linear quality (the goal to be reached) and a chaotic quality (the intervening and unsuspected block). Those attracted to challenge enjoy overcoming problems through direct, sometimes impulsive (and impetuous) actions. Alteration is more important than rearranging. The act of breaking up anything stagnant or clotting is more important than following whatever flows as a result.

Embodiments in Relationships: Competitive; risk-taking; critical of status quo. May enjoy creating challenges just to overcome them. Prefer acts of commitment over conversation. Also, there is a keenness on the quality of "alterity" and "otherness"; that is, a recognition that something, a person, or process is radically alien to yourself or to the current habits and norms that surround your circumstances.

Embodiments in Career, Professions: Debating; legal or justice-related work; supporting the underdog or downtrodden; critic; enjoy working with start-ups. As a leader, you may be prone to say, "I want us to take on another challenge that will engage and motivate as many of us as possible. What is our next big challenge? How soon can we take it on?"

Attraction in Work Style: The strongest attraction is likely for finding and addressing risk factors (deadweight, stagnation, and unhealthy elements) in any setting. The desire to assess becomes the basis for mounting a strategy for reducing those risks, especially if these risks appear impossible to others. On a team, this manifests as the one who can get ideas off the table if there is stagnation. You also can inspire others by laying down a challenge.

Cautions in Working/Relating with Others: Others may feel you do not take the time to consider their ideas. They may not even see things as a challenge. Be careful not to get so focused on your own pressing goals that you lose sight of the longer-term goals of the relationship, the team, or the community.

The Challenge (Stuck in this Space): The growth opportunity is to recognize that not everything has to be approached as a challenge. It helps to take a more paced approach, one required for maintaining a strategy over time. The tendency is to only see making something happen (action) as critical without considering that you may need to build capacity, inquire and listen, and take time with others. You may blurt out or say things you might regret later. Others may complain, "Great energy and momentum, but has everyone seen the plan"? or "When are you going to learn to pick your battles"? or "Sometimes it seems like you have a chip on your shoulder or a vendetta."

Corrections: Seek out the negotiating and discerning energy, or learn how to adapt this attitude when presenting your new idea, challenge, or action plan. Learn how to work well and negotiate strategies with others. This attitude can help you slow down and see the big picture so you can pick the "right battle" to fight at the right time. This way, you can conserve your energy rather than wasting it on what may not be the best bet right now.

Affirmations: I effectively consider others' perspectives, select a strategy that works best for myself and others, and address the challenges we face at the same time. I calmly abide in patience. I find and enjoy the harmony I see among those I live and work with.

Treasures: Abide in Momentous events (the richness of life) and Fulfillment. Practice patience, desire, and yearning.

INTENDING

"Carpe diem."
~LATIN: "SEIZE THE DAY."

"It is when we act freely, for the sake of the action itself rather than for ulterior motives, that we learn to become more than what we were."

~MIHALY CSIKSZENTMIHALYI, *FLOW: THE PSYCHOLOGY OF OPTIMAL EXPERIENCE*

Synonyms: accomplishing, achieving, acting, activating, animating, articulating, deciding, directing, driving, endeavoring, executing, intervening, laboring, leading, moving (forward), operating, performing, powering, realizing, resolving (to take action), responding, strategizing, time shaping (also "Time Shaping")

Primary Attraction: Enjoying the ability to make things happen, to turn ideas into reality, and to act. The Attraction is for articulating a vision. Manifests as leadership when leadership is defined as moving groups and projects into the future. You sense an opportunity and can be decisive when others are requiring somebody to make an important decision. In reviewing the synonyms above, note how they all require a quality of intention that results in acting toward time as it is anticipated in the future.

Description: You are primarily oriented to the future, seeing what exists and filling the gap between current and unmet needs and future satisfaction. With this energy, you make things happen with immediacy or set things in motion and watch—preferably with an open mind—as events take shape and unfold. You view time as primarily linear and moving in one direction. You don't look back. The tendency is to take action now and ask questions later, taking every opportunity to set wheels turning. Accordingly, all time-management tools are useful in so far as they serve that purpose. To-do lists exist so you can scratch off each accomplishment from the list and move on.

Embodiments in Relationships: Tend to take charge; decisiveness; ready to take action and move things along or ahead (sometimes without seeing others' needs or perspectives).

Embodiments in Career, Professions: Management, leadership, or position of relative power or influence. You enjoy work where you can see immediate results or where work on a process is clearly tied to outcomes and the ability to influence those outcomes. As a leader, you may be prone to say, "This is where we are headed, and I need to know each of you is on board to make that happen. The time is now. Who is with me?"

Attraction in Work Style: The strongest attraction is toward goal setting, directing program or service delivery, and getting programs, products, or services into the hands of those who can use them. There is a desire to see programs or services used, that people react positively to you, and that outcomes are tracked and measured. You see each step as following a logical sequence (for example, Plan→Do→ Check (Study, Monitor)→Act), and will often emphasize the outcome, perhaps in hard numbers or return-on-investment (ROI) ratios. These then become tools for bolstering and strategizing next steps or programs in the future. (You may think, "Why bother acting if there is not a good chance that it will yield an intended result"?)

Cautions in Working with Others: Your plan may not always be the best for everyone on the team. You may come across as inconsiderate, dismissive, or insensitive. It is best to take a consultative role with others who are more sensitive to surrounding conditions or others' needs and ideas. While your ideas may be the best, they cannot become reality without building capacity with others and understanding their willingness to change. Others may see you as a bull in a china shop, asking, "Who died and made you the boss"? or "Can you slow down so we can regroup"?

The Challenge (Stuck in this Space): The growth opportunity lies in recognizing the surrounding conditions or context of actions and programs. Like the neighboring Attraction of Catalyzing (see above), there is a tendency to either (a) forge ahead when it may not be time yet ("I need to get things moving") or when other factors have not fallen into place; or (b) to immediately dismiss something ("I don't have time for this") because it does not fit the intention. A key difference between Catalyzing and Intending involves repetition, perseverance, and commitment. For intending, repeated efforts that do not result in cherished goals may lead to burnout and disillusionment. In contrast, for Catalyzing, only one effort is more likely to be sufficient.

Corrections: See action sequences from the perspective of nurturing or bringing out everyone's potential. Learn how to adapt this attitude before you get started and as you move ahead into action. Learn how to gather lots of information to make your case. Ultimately, make it your goal to discern the best time to act, knowing that the best time considers the big picture.

Affirmations: My actions create a healthy (workplace, relationship) because I work with and for those I (serve, love). The positive results of this attitude are already starting to show up. I stop to savor my life. Life is precious.

Treasures: Practice questing to overcome a challenge (look for movement), experience completion, show zeal, look forward to more (Optimism), and gain insight into resistance.

COORDINATING

"From a drop of water, a logician could predict an Atlantic or Niagara."

~SIR ARTHUR CONAN DOYLE, BRITISH AUTHOR
OF SHERLOCK HOLMES STORIES (1859–1930)

Synonyms: arranging, calculating, calibrating, computing, engineering, forecasting, gauging, managing, modeling, planning, plotting, preparing, problem-solving, programming, regulating, sequencing, working out, technologizing, modernizing

Primary Attraction: Enjoying a focus on the details and mechanics necessary to make things work, solve a problem, work things out, advance a field of knowledge. Providing the template or game plan that shows step by step how certain actionable goals lead to others in a sequence. Emphasis on logic and calculations so activities, endeavors, journeys, and projects move along and are done with efficiency. Through engineering, one foresees logical outcomes of early actions others neglect. They think more "down the road" than would happen through pure intending and time shaping. At the same time, they like to hear or see things "whirring," moving into some assembly, taking form piece by piece.

Description: Engineering has a dual orientation to some target in the future (like intending or Time Shaping) and methods (routines, schedules) that can be manipulated or programmed to achieve a targeted outcome. The tendency, however, is slightly more to the methods (tools, guides) you can use than to actions themselves. Less energy is spent on getting out "into the world" and taking action than on preparing, organizing, and imagining different scenarios based on inputs, logic, and outputs. With this Attraction, you like to tinker with things but are not likely to get so absorbed in the tinkering as to lose sight of the objective.

Embodiments in Relationships: Tend to believe that things should fall into a sequence or pattern. Enjoy planning events or maintaining routines and being appreciated for that, or otherwise proving to yourself that the designed plan is effective or efficient. In relationships, those with this Attraction enjoy seeing how events and occasions unfold as planned or without a hitch.

Embodiments in Career, Professions: Engineers; computer programming; software developer; profiling; detective; event planning. As a leader, you may be prone to say, "I have laid out the key objectives, milestones, and timelines for this project. Can everyone confirm their role as we proceed and when they will deliver"?

Attraction in Work Style: A strong attraction for understanding and targeting the intervening logics and paths between stages of any process, for example, the stage between knowing a customer's or client's needs and then selecting the right service or product. You are likely to enjoy any logic that allows you to see how a customer or client profile identifies their needs, which leads to certain programs that can be monitored to ensure results are obtained. You have a similar interest in planning and targeting proximal outcomes that can logically influence long-term goals.

The Challenge (Stuck in this Space): The greatest challenge may be too strong of an emphasis on control and low tolerance for "error" in the system. There are a host of unforeseeable, historical, and maturational factors that come into play between the time something is delivered and an expected outcome. This can be difficult for those working with people, complex systems, or with the "messiness" of social or political systems.

Cautions in Working with Others: This Attraction is probably the most biased to the "science" of things and less open to viewing life as an "art." However, many situations in life may be based on personal idiosyncrasies and unique aspirations of others. Accordingly, others may not be interested in or able to understand the logic of coordinating and engineering. The caution is to avoid withdrawing or feeling alienated when this happens. Others may judge you or complain, "You are a 'know-it-all'" or "Why do we always have to do things your way"? or "You are too rigid or micromanaging."

Corrections: Negotiate or adapt the orientation that allows you to have more appreciation for the social and creative aspects of life as an "art." Be mindful that events may not always follow a logical sequence because there are people involved with different viewpoints and agendas.

Affirmations: I successfully combine logic and action to create an effective strategy that works for me and others. Everything "just clicks" or falls into place. I let go of control. I easily forgive and ask for forgiveness.

Treasures: Abide in Effortlessness and Ordinariness, look for intelligence and perfection, and see grace in the way things work.

CENTERING

*"A place for everything
and everything in its place."*

~Benjamin Franklin, American statesman
and inventor (1706–1790)

Synonyms: abiding, anchoring, assuring, calming, establishing, focusing, grounding, leveling, maintaining, organizing, poising, rooting, securing, settling, sourcing, stabilizing, supporting, underpinning (also "Organizing")

Primary Attraction: Bringing patience and order to activities. Enjoying the capacity to develop a system, container, routine, or logical framework to make sure that everything stays on track, follows timelines, meets milestones, and ultimately reaches objectives. With this attraction, one formulates routines and schedules that create a sense of stability and sustainability to projects and relationships.

Description: You enjoy routines and the beauty of allowing things to unfold and transition over time. You like seeing your plans unfold. You approach occasions in terms of project and time management. Accordingly, the tendency is to view time in terms of packaged increments (hours make up days, days make up weeks, and so on). By keeping things organized—through routines and schedules—you can plan the sequence or flow of activities. For example, you estimate that the family needs two months to plan for the next vacation and three weeks to get things ready, so you prepare items and actions in advance (or at least spend a good amount of time thinking about it).

Embodiments in Relationships: Enjoy organizing more than creativity. Likely to prefer clear and hard boundaries between work activities, private time with family, time with friends, and other life events. Those having this attraction will likely enjoy routines, loyalty, commitments, and adhering to expectations and norms. As you embody the Soulful Capacities, you will likely be a great listener and maintain a sense of poise and serenity while others may be more reactive.

Embodiments in Career, Professions: Project management; working in "hard" sciences of physics and chemistry; operations; administrative positions; chief of staff. As a leader, you may be prone to say, "The system has been set up for success. Now, all we need is to make sure we follow the plan together. Can we each confirm that now"?

Attraction in Work Style: The attraction is likely for keeping all aspects of work in an ordered filing system where everything is easy to locate. You have an interest in work that mimics or uses organized systems, including filing and logic/workflows, and different aspects of any educational sequence.

Cautions in Working with Others: A strong attraction here will lead to difficulties with others who have strong attractions in any other area. For example, working with a highly driven "time shaper" may require that you surrender plans to do things properly. An "innovator" may require open-mindedness when you know there is only one way. Working with a "nurturer" may lead you to feel like your system or way of doing things is not taken seriously. Others may complain that you take things too seriously or that you need to have more flexibility.

The Challenge (Stuck in this Space): Major challenges are the unpredictable aspects of working with others, new systems, and instabilities. This includes accidents, critical incidents, traumas, and unsuspected changes in policy. Sometimes it is necessary to move quickly when there is insufficient data or a fully organized plan. Other times, certain constituencies and social processes lead to lapses. Those strongly attracted to organizing need to prepare for these.

Corrections: Patience is a key virtue that comes with organizing. The correction is to adapt the middle point between your position and those you are having difficulties with. If you are struggling with others, learn how to adapt that attitude.

Affirmations: I am flexible in my ways of organizing so that I both adapt to situations and create the best plan for success. I am confident that everything has its right time to show up to make the whole plan work. I enjoy just being spontaneous. Life is awesome, and I am humbled by it all.

Treasures: Abide in Coherence and Adoration, and appreciate peace, placement, and the order of things. Practice attention, faith, listening, and silence.

DISCERNING

"Truth uttered before its time is dangerous."

~MENCIUS, CHINESE PHILOSOPHER
AND SAGE (371–289 BC)

Synonyms: attending, coaching, communicating, connecting, consulting, deliberating, discussing, distinguishing, empathizing, heeding, listening, mediating, negotiating, recognizing (as in giving someone recognition), regarding, relating, responding, sympathizing, understanding (also "Negotiating")

Note: Also attracted to states of heedfulness, diplomacy, using discretion, tactfulness, prudence, considerateness

Primary Attraction: An ability to communicate effectively, work with opposing perspectives, and negotiate an optimal solution. One likes to provide needed and detailed attention to the overall quality of things (events, projects) and can play a "public relations" or diplomatic role. The desire is to both have things meet the quality standards for the satisfaction of as many people, family, friends, or stakeholders as possible and to enjoy the process of improving quality.

Description: Those with this attraction derive great satisfaction from discerning the right time to act, especially in the realm of human relationships. With discerning or negotiating energy, you approach life in terms of discerning what is best for community, peace, and building teams, coalitions, or alignments. In its purest form, time is constructed primarily through relationships and does not exist as something independent of people working in community. You understand that everything is subject to interpretation and translation. Accordingly, you take the position of always working *toward* a solution by finding the right mix of people to bring together, network, and form a relationship. The goal is a translational strategy for improving health, effectiveness, or success.

Embodiments in Relationships: Enjoy talking, discussing, coming up with solutions together with others. Prefer dialog and conversation to acts of service.

Embodiments in Career, Professions: Counseling, therapy, consulting, coaching, advisor role. As a leader, you may be prone to say, "I believe in each of you, your talents and strengths, and I know you well enough to know you can work together to help each other bring those strengths out. Who would like to talk about the strengths they see in one of their coworkers? Please take your time."

Attraction in Work Style: The attraction is for social interest, social support, and building social protective factors. Successful programs or projects can be launched by those who can negotiate with all the other attractions. Those who enjoy negotiating will likely help to gather information about risks, needs, and interests and then design and deliver options from all perspectives. No one component of a product or service will be as attractive as the ability to use tools for communication and discerning processes that enhance communication. Communication/marketing tools are probably best administered by those with this attraction.

Cautions in Working with Others: The major caution is the ability to take sides without appearing wishy-washy, noncommittal, two-faced, or untrustworthy. Too strong an attraction here can lead to sacrificing any internal sense of self or values to "please the crowd" or maintain an allegiance that betrays the soul. Others may complain that you lack backbone or can't take a stand as you may be more willing to make compromises than dictate a solution.

The Challenge (Stuck in this Space): Be careful of the need to have others depend on you. Once someone with this Attraction leaves a team, things may fall apart, especially if the team depended on that person's conflict management skills. Goodness in life depends on an inclusive social network. Those who negotiate need to know that sustainability of a system requires other perspectives. These come into play *after* negotiation is complete. Those attracted here should accommodate Challenging and Intending (Time Shaping) energies lest the system becomes unstable.

Corrections: Negotiating energy or diplomacy is very close to discerning the right time to do or say something and reading the current phase or transition point in a relationship. Part of discernment includes knowing when the energies or Attractions of others need to come to the foreground. Not everything has to be negotiated or settled just yet.

Affirmations: I am sought after to address the strengths of those I (work with, am friends with, love), and together we negotiate an effective plan. I enjoy each moment. I am fulfilled.

Treasures: Abide in Resonance and Patience and appreciate service, harmony, reciprocity, and justice. Practice compassion, hospitality, and remembrance of helpful mentors and teachers and their qualities.

POTENTIATING

*"There is a time for everything, and a season
for every activity under the heavens ..."*

~KING SOLOMON, ECCLESIASTES 3:1

*"In every heart there is a god of flowers just waiting
to come out of its cloud and lift its wings."*

~MARY OLIVER, AMERICAN POET (1935–2019)

Synonyms: assisting, boosting, cultivating, developing, educating, encouraging, entraining with, facilitating, furthering, giving, growing, intuiting, joining with, nourishing, nurturing, offering, promoting, propagating, treasuring (also anything associated with seeing and promoting the conditions that bring about change, including having a "big picture" or surrounding "context" insight; wisdom) (also "Nurturing")

Primary Attraction: Understanding that things take time and cultivating the best conditions for something to grow. Having intuitive insight into Nurturing Conditions, the big picture, and the many relationships involved in a successful effort (in health, work, or relationships). Advocating for well-being and inclusiveness and assuring all perspectives feel cared for.

Description: This energy is sensitive to life's rhythms and transitions. Time emerges according to the conditions of the situation. You can "read" the state or climate of others and often have good intuition. You are least likely to require an external measure to validate your perceptions (for example, an assessment or survey) because of your innate ability to interpret others' concerns and hopes. Like the negotiating or diplomatic attraction, "nurturers" are oriented to others but more focused on the greatest good. They are also less focused on success and more so on finding the right fit for things to grow.

Embodiments in Relationships: Enjoy helping, being of service, domestic chores, cooking and cleaning, taking care of the home.

Embodiments in Career, Professions: Healthcare and affiliated professions, nursing, teaching, health coaching, family caregiver, gardening, parenting, agriculture, hospitality, cooking, volunteering. People with this Attraction make good facilitators, trainers, and health coaches and may be most drawn to delivering social services. As a leader, you may be prone to bring the team together for a luncheon or retreat and say, "The potential for success is great, and I am inspired by how each of you can lead us all to success. I would like each of you to talk about your own vision for success. Who would like to go first"?

Attraction in Work Style: Creates a fit between all the different components that make a healthy or successful family, community, or organization: the people, the program, the delivery system, and the deliverers. The emphasis is less on outcomes and more on process. You intrinsically enjoy the process of cultivating (putting together) anything that can help others. You can easily "let go" of any tool, object, program, or approach that does not fit and can be the first to detect new trends are moving in a different direction.

Cautions in Working with Others: One may become idealistic and expect others to have the same level of compassion or a nurturing attitude. It helps to be aware that the pace of others—team players (or organizational elements)—may not always be in sync with each other. That is, just because you see how things are working and can communicate that perspective to others does not mean that others on the team see eye to eye. The tendency to please everyone could also result in stagnation.

The Challenge (Stuck in this Space): You may get lost in the process of building capacity and relationships and neglect to take action when sudden or significant effort is called for. The challenge is opposite to that of Intending (Time Shaping), where you may be ready to take action and cause something to happen but neglect the context. You may do a good job of getting everyone involved but fail to articulate a clear vision or action plan. The complaint here is that while you help foster conditions for growth, you may not be well organized (see Centering or Organizing) or strategic (see Time Shaping) enough to create a real-world, sustainable effort. With a strong attraction in this area, be careful not to overcommit to others (for example, being on too many teams or committees).

Corrections: Review the strengths of each of the perspectives described in this feedback section. Bring different players and perspectives together to discuss. Your strength is that you can facilitate meetings and dialog to bring out the greater good of the whole team that different players will not see from their own perspectives.

Affirmations: I have the wisdom to create the conditions for effective endeavors. I know when to follow through with decisive action. I am filled with optimism. I rise to the occasion.

Treasures: Abide in Preciousness and Savoring. Appreciate beauty, goodness, regeneration, and flowering. Practice nurturing and kindness.

CRAFTING

*"Do not go where the path may lead,
go instead where there is no path and leave a trail."*

~RALPH WALDO EMERSON, AMERICAN AUTHOR,
POET, AND PHILOSOPHER (1803–1882)

*"To invent, you need a good imagination
and a pile of junk."*

~THOMAS ALVA EDISON,
AMERICAN INVENTOR (1847–1931)

Synonyms: authoring, coloring, creating, customizing, dancing, designing, editing, expressing, invoking, inventing, jiggling, molding, playing, sculpturing, shading, shaking, shaping, tailoring, tweaking, writing

Primary Attraction: Drawn to customizing (adapting and designing) things as a joy in and of itself and often and also in such a way as to have meaning, entertainment, and the most enjoyable delight (but not necessarily practical use) by others. Drawing upon and combining the strengths of Opening and Potentiating to create new art, products, tools, programs (or adaptations) that will be attractive to others. Unlike pure dancing and innovation—which enjoys creating for its own sake—crafting implies that the created tool will be meaningful, delightful, or enjoyable to at least one other person.

Description: Attraction to be an artisan, a craftsperson, someone who enjoys the creative process, often because you can apply media and design elements to fashion a "piece" that addresses an aesthetic or social need or both. The objective is to create something that others will both enjoy and use in the future. With this Attraction, you may be a consultant who advises on where to place certain items within a scheme or when is the best time to run an event.

Embodiments in Relationships: Enjoy playing with others; leisure; finding opportunities for dance, music, playing games. Prefer quality "together time" over acts of service or housework.

Embodiments in Career, Professions: Handicrafts or working with industrial arts, materials, and fabrics; application development; drafting; architectural design; construction; landscaping. As a leader, you may be prone to say, "We can create something beautiful and meaningful by tapping into the creative juices of the team. Let's take all the time we need to find that which is greater than the sum of each of us."

Attraction in Work Style: You are attracted to knowing the details of different design options and manipulating or fashioning them in a way that serves others' needs. Linear time is relaxed. The emphasis is on customizing or tweaking a product so that it works *for* the need. Time has a quality of ongoingness and flow; the goal is to bring everyone into the same rhythm. You have the capacity to bring in disparate elements (for example, an old curriculum) that others may have ignored and make them work with the overall scheme of things. Those with this Attraction are an asset to any team because of their ability to work with different perspectives when it comes to creating a workable program.

The Challenge (Stuck in this Space): The challenge is to stay grounded in goals and timelines. You may be able to develop or fashion something that suits the needs of others. However, even after all that work has gone on, the result may still not be actionable. You can get frustrated when your "work" or effort lies on a shelf or it is not recognized for the creative effort that went into it.

Cautions in Working with Others: You may have difficulty seeing the logic or logical outcome of an effort that extends beyond the creative work. Because the intention is often to take others' ideas into consideration, you may have difficulty when original ideas are further adapted and modified to fit someone else's agenda. This "drift" away from originality can lead to frustration. The creator feels that the intent of the program was misunderstood or even corrupted. Others may complain that your need for originality or "putting your unique stamp" on something hurts the process or outcome.

Corrections: Review the strengths of Engineering and adapt your attitude toward logic and problem solving. If there is frustration, remember that there are ups and downs in any creative process.

Affirmations: I flow with changes that occur over time and have faith that the outcome will be just right for myself and others. Life is effortless. I calmly take things one day at a time.

Treasures: Abide in Poignancy (meaning) and Release. Appreciate creativity and transcending dichotomies. Practice imagination, connections, openness, and looking for the mystery (the x factor).

SYNTHESIZING

*"It is our destiny as males and females to work together
to restore our original state of connection rooted in
mutuality and devotion to cultivate human well-being."*

~BELL HOOKS, AMERICAN AUTHOR, INTELLECTUAL, FEMINIST
(1952–2021)

Synonyms: balancing, broadening, consolidating, deepening, expanding, heightening, integrating, process synthesizing, seeing the pattern, sharpening, spanning, traversing, unifying, transpersonalizing, delighting (also "Integrating")

Note: Synthesizing also works in relationship to the other Attractions through rediscovering, recharging, reenacting, recalibrating, reallocating, reviving, and reinventing. Synthesizing is not the same as having a meta-perspective of transcendence. Instead, any of the Attractions can bring self-transcendence through cultivation of the Soulful Capacities.

Primary Attraction: There are two types of Synthesizing Attractions: One is the ability to take the perspective of different sides (type I); the other is to maintain a truly integrated position without taking perspectives (type II). You know if you're a type II based on whether you tended to always take the middle ("3" or "4") response options in the questionnaire. With either Attraction, you can see the other eight approaches from a center point and bring these together for synthesis. You also can pull different pieces together into a single frame so that everyone can see how the different pieces work together. This capacity can be very helpful when there are different "silos" of operations in any group, family, or organization.

Description: Integrating can be like a "jack-of-all-trades, master of none," with a sense of delight and ownership. It is like one is a master of being a jack-of-all-trades. The tendency is to see potential alliances and conflicts as well as potential successes and pitfalls. You enjoy understanding and addressing all types of communication issues. Accordingly, time has a bidirectional quality. Type I Integration can fully adapt the future-oriented vision of Intending (Time Shaping) but also sees the importance of taking time to Potentiate and build Nurturing Conditions. With Integration, you enjoy bringing the past and future together for review. Similarly, they can go back-and-forth between structure and routine and also throw themselves fully into innovation and openness. Type II Integration is more likely to take an observer role and find a center point.

Embodiments: May adapt any or all the embodiments listed in the other Attractions. It is best to review specific items on the questionnaire and find those you liked the most. Use these to better discern other primary Attractions.

Embodiments in Relationships: Enjoy bringing out the best in all people in the family or community.

Embodiments in Career, Professions: Being on a multidisciplinary team, working on projects involving multiple stakeholders, or being the strategist or consultant who helps everyone see the big picture. As a leader, you may be prone to set up a meeting and say, "Here is where we came from, here is where I think we are headed; and I would like each of you share how you think we are going to get there. You can use any style or method to express your vision."

Attraction in Work Style: Attracted to anything that requires synthesis: taking a systems perspective, coordinating efforts, building on previous efforts rather than re-creating the wheel, taking advantage of preexisting synergies, and forming a coalition. This includes being a "boundary spanner" and gathering information from "silos," synthesis of data, using communication tools as a way to assess and listen to perspectives, and reviewing processes from time to time to make sure everyone is on board.

Cautions in Working with Others: Integrating energy is great to have in any family, group, or team—unless you have too many people or projects with complex, diverse, or competing aspects. Those attracted to synthesizing can get overwhelmed—and hurt their health—because of a compulsion to integrate features that cannot or should not be integrated. The issue here is that the group can run into all the problems of the other types, including stagnation, conflict, and failure to plan for problems, among others. Someone will need to get the integrative energy off the center-point position so that things can move in some direction. Others may complain, "Make up your mind" or "Stop trying to be everything for everybody" or "Stay in your lane" or "You are a chameleon; it is hard to get to know you."

The Challenge (Stuck in this Space): Challenges include high distractibility, multitasking, or being pulled in too many directions and getting overwhelmed. Type I Integrators may think they see the "big picture" when in actuality they only see many different pieces. They assume that they see everything, but the task remains to bring players to the table. Type II Integrators are the most noncommittal of any of the nine types. Others can see you as two-faced. In truth, they really cannot make up their minds, or they are overly cautious about balancing too many things.

Corrections: Review the strengths of all the perspectives, especially their most extreme manifestations. Take a back seat, and let the right set or composition of elements present themselves. Find allies from neighboring areas with which you are having difficulty. For example, if you have difficulties with Time Shapers, find an Engineer or Challenger to help you get the message across.

Affirmations: I gradually and successfully bring people together for the good of the whole. I remain open to what unfolds without having to do anything myself. Everything falls into place, or not, and I am OK with it either way.

Treasures: There may or may not be a tendency toward one single Treasure. Instead, coming from the center of the mandala, Synthesizers come to know about their journey by noticing which Treasures happen to show up. Appreciate awareness, focus, and purity. Appreciate the values of self-sufficiency and the uniqueness of each element in an interdependent set of elements. Instead of being caught up in the world as a swirl or kaleidoscope, see it more as a mosaic with unique and colorful elements, each one contributing to the whole.

Summary of Nine Attractions and Expressions in Relatively Low or High Soulful Capacity

If my main Attraction is:	I prefer to do one or more of these:	If my soulful capacity tends toward higher levels	If my soulful capacity tends toward lower levels	Alternate affirmation:
Opening / Innovating	open, create, diverge	Immersing oneself fully in life; discovering; experiencing true wonder and awe; life is exciting and spontaneous	Not in touch with reality; out of sync with others; too much into oneself or one's own ideas and impulses	My creativity inspires me to explore the world, the practices, interests, and feelings of others
Catalyzing/ Challenging	catalyze, risk, disrupt	Feeling fulfilled by one's calling or destiny; vitally engaged in the world through activity	Not paced, deliberate, or nuanced; being a victim; an unhealthy renegade	I embrace the challenges of life in ways that center me in the moment
Intending/ Time Shaping	intend, drive, motivate, activate, inspire	A sense of positive movement, optimism, inspiration from being here and now; flowing; confidence in being	Narcissistic; bullies others; insensitive; careless; over the top; alternately, impulsive... fools rush in where angels fear to tread	I am relaxed and whole in my day-to-day activities
Coordinating/ Engineering	coordinate, calculate, calibrate	Effortless enjoyment of life's details; seeing patterns; bringing things into perspective; skillful means	Intolerant; perfectionistic; micromanaging	Everything that happens is perfect for my journey
Centering/ Organizing	center, stabilize, ground	Relishing in the form of things; aesthetics; symmetry; able to adore the coherence of the world; present and centered	Rigidity; difficulty with creative elements; stuck in the mud; overly serious	I am open to new moments in my life that befriend and teach me

If my main Attraction is:	I prefer to do one or more of these:	If my soulful capacity tends toward higher levels	If my soulful capacity tends toward lower levels	Alternate affirmation:
Discerning/ Negotiating	discern, communicate, use diplomacy, harmonize	Excitement in working with and joining with others; knowing what is right and when it is right; bringing people together in harmony; love; and love resonating with life	Lack of backbone; two-sided; schizoid; people pleaser; wishy-washy	I see clearly and with the wisdom of the heart
Potentiating/ Nurturing	potentiate, cultivate, facilitate, frame context	Fully aware of the beauty of life; able to capture and savor precious moments and help others to do the same; always seeing what is becoming, the big picture, and nurturing others	Doormat; codependent; failure to act; failure to defend oneself; neglects one's own needs; over-committed	I give to others as also I give to and nurture myself
Crafting	dance, design, customize	The world has a joyful, almost fun-like quality; enjoys and supports the quality of things; finding ways to be in rhythm with and synchronizing to cocreate with others and with life	Stuck in originality; too precious; terminally unique; struggling artist; "no one understands"	I am whole and able to feel deep joy from my work with others
Synthesizing/ Integrating	synthesize, unify	Seeing wholeness and unity in life; innately knowing how things connect; seeing the pattern and helping others to see it as well	Attention deficit; stagnation; chameleon-like; lack of intimacy; disconnected	There is enough time for everything and for everything there is enough time

Contemplation (QfP 3-3): Gaze at Your Map, Study It, Revise It

The greatest achievements in human history have all been made possible by the science of cartography.

~KEN JENNINGS (FROM *MAPHEAD: CHARTING THE WIDE, WEIRD WORLD OF GEOGRAPHY WONKS*)

Cartography is the study and science of map making and map using. As Ken Jennings and others have pointed out, the history of the world is replete with the continual updating of maps. The result of every true exploration is some change in a map, if not a complete revision. The Quest for Presence Inventory™ is only an approximation, a starting point, just like any other map. As explained in depth in *QfP Book 1*, the map is not the terrain. I hope that you now have something tangible to work with as you move into the terrain.

RECONNOITER (Observe the Region)

1. Do you align, agree, or resonate with the interpretation feedback on your Attraction Feedback forms?

2. Did you review the feedback forms for all Attractions in your general area?

3. What do you think you are really attracted to right now in your life?

PREPARATION (Gather Key Clues)

4. What are "in the works," "cooking," and "about to take place" for you?

5. Which aspects of your life do you consider as "stable," "steady," "tried and true"?

6. What needs to get done, or what are you on the brink of launching?

7. What aspects of your personality do you need to let loose? What do you need to break free from? What routine do you need to step outside of?

ACTION (Walk the Perimeter)

8. Who else in your life can you ask to complete the QFPI™? Go ahead and do so, and compare notes.

9. Remember that sharing is an important part of the Q∫P journey. What can you share from this tool that will help you in your work, relationships, family, or other key area (such as hobbies, vacation, leisure)? Go ahead and do so, and see what happens next.

The Folds: Details and Examples

An Ode to Friends

There was no clear beginning
to this conversation
and it doesn't matter anyway.

You just keep following each other:

the news, this joke, that secret,
your insight, her fear,
that memory, your vision,
his mistake, your forgiveness,
and then the gratitude,

and the listening to
the silence
together

as two souls awaken

There was no clear end
to this conversation
and it doesn't matter anyway.

~J.B.

The art of conversation, of skillfully having a sincere and authentic dialog, can bring great insight, promote healing, and lead to awakening. But what is there to talk about? And with who? Well, we can always talk about the weather. In many ways, talking about the weather is also talking about time—what happened, what is happening, what will happen. And we can talk about the weather with anyone. It is quite simple.

In QfP and your own journey, I encourage you to get with others and share about your Attraction. Ask each other, "What has your journey been like? What is changing, emerging, unfolding in your life?" And take the time to listen. Listen for the enfolding—how the Radiant Forces and Soulful Capacities are always there, coming to the surface in our stories. Also, ask others who have taken the QFPI™, "How does each Attraction show up in your life—in how you work; how you play; how you relate to your partner, spouse, significant other, boss, or coworker?" And take the time to listen.

In this section of Book 3—"The Folds: Details and Examples"— you will find dozens of examples or fragments taken from diverse Attraction stories. I hope you find at least one that you can relate to. But then, go and tell someone about why it resonated with you. I offer a simple trick.

Start by talking about the weather. For example, the coming of autumn or spring (a segue into Nurturing Conditions); or a recent event, such as a thunderstorm, heavy snow, hurricane, or tornado (a segue into Chaos); or the cold, the heat, or cloud formations. It is a magical thing about life—and our connections with each other—how talking about the weather can further our quest for presence.

CHAPTER 4

Portraits

An Ode to Our Differences

I don't want anything to come between us.

So, let's just agree that found time is never lost; instead
of that out worn flag: lost time is never found.

Yes, lots of endless time or timelessness or endlessness
or just the ever.

There we are, you and I, dancing like angels on the
head of a pin.
Moving in different ways all over. All at the same time.

You swirl and break open.
    I gather the pieces and plant them.
You spy the shape of an octopus in some gallivanting
galaxy and take off.
    I watch in awe.
You collect the fruits of your delicious mistakes.
    I drink in from biting them and forget what
      brought us here.
I start opening like branches from the trunk that was
once the pin.
    You alight on one of me.

We fight for attention until we're exhausted from
   laughing that we are the totality. This tree, that
   branch, you, the stars, those tentacles reaching
   down to nudge you into flight...
again.

I recognize the arc of your murmuration, each upon
   each, within each, for each.

You enter my broken heart.
      I watch in awe.

We are never alone when we age like this backwards
   into the germ root of our longing; or is it forward
   into the longing for our germ root?

This maddening spiral that is our dear home.

      This place where nothing comes between us.

~J.B.

This chapter shares brief examples of individuals who have taken the Quest for Presence Inventory (QFPI™), sometimes on multiple occasions over a period of months, and then shared their experiences. Every time, in the moment of their sharing, we become friends. Many of these individuals had also taken "The Quest for Presence" online workshop with me.

While there is a general tendency for consistency in ratings over time, almost everyone describes subtle changes or insights that come from taking the questionnaire and reflecting on the feedback forms (see the previous chapter). Also, to drive home the point that this system is not about "typing" you, I provide examples of how each of the

Attractions has expressed themselves in my life. We all have access to each of these attractive tendencies. In other words, it is better to grasp the universality or common humanity that lives within the diversity of human personality than to only focus on, and reify, what makes us so different from one another. We can all take the perspective of others because we all, at one time or another, have a sense of these expressions.

There is another important feature to emphasize. The QFPI™ is more like a Rorschach test, a tool whose value lies in how each individual orients toward and gives their own interpretation of the results. Many times, the insight occurs not from the actual score or feedback received but how the individual feels about the test, the items, the *process* of taking the questionnaire, and the *process* of interpreting results. This is why I ask people to review the Attraction Matrix Commitment Statements ("I am committed to ..."), found on page 39, before taking the QFPI™. It also helps to review these commitment statements after taking the survey.

Alan: "Does Not Grab Me, or Does It?"

Sometimes, in taking the QFPI™ and receiving feedback, people don't resonate with it at all. They find it ephemeral and struggle to pin down what the feedback means. Alan, a middle-aged counselor with many years of spiritual study, shared, "The survey did not make sense to me on either time that I took it." Alan had taken the QFPI™ twice over a nine-month span. "I honestly am having trouble answering the questions."

Alan had taken the Q*f*P online workshop, but he noted that at the time, "I was not very present and did not connect deeply with the course teachings. The concepts intrigued me, but I did not get it."

When I asked Alan to share more, he mentioned that he had reflected recently that he needed "more structure and regular routines in my life." In particular, he wanted to introduce some new practices and tools to his clients. It dawned on him that as he was taking the QFPI™, he saw this need directly reflected in specific items.

"I bumped into that topic in several pairs [items 2, 6, 9, and 11] when I retook the assessment," Alan said. "I noticed that the statements … that I assumed I would most closely agree with—from a 'personality' standpoint, I guess, from a 'that's me' standpoint—were the statements describing a more flexible personality when it comes to structure."

Examples of those item pairs include:

I enjoy work that has order and procedures.
I enjoy work that involves risks and surprises.

I prefer to work with known methods and established guidelines.
I prefer to play and experiment with new ideas and explore the unknown.

The first statement in each pair is oriented toward Form, while the second is oriented toward Chaos. Alan described a desire to have more structure in his work than he felt his personality allowed: "My current yearning (perhaps it is a fear) seems to be more in line with the statements that describe a person wanting reliable/predictable structure, order, path, plan, etc., in their life's work."

Alan was struggling with his strong tendency toward being creative and having diverse ways of expressing that creativity in his work with clients. At the same time, he needed more regularity or routine. He wanted this and was also afraid that it would limit him.

Alan's final QFPI™ score on both of his completions showed that he was clearly in the Crafting quadrant. He was, in fact, yearning to design something new to help his clients. Reviewing the Corrections section of the Attractions feedback for Crafting was very helpful for Alan. "Review the strengths of Engineering and adapt their attitude toward logic and problem solving," the form suggests. Alan realized that he needed a collaborator, someone to bounce ideas off so he could further ground his talents and design a curriculum and tools. This would allow him to negotiate his ambivalence.

Alan was having difficulty committing to taking action toward a particular project, choosing a behavior that would allow him to take the first step (Time Shaping) toward his new creation. Instead of seeing the relationship between Form and Chaos as one of tension and conflict, I invited him to see that a mystery was unfolding and that his work was part of what was emerging. The Treasures section of the feedback form for Crafting suggested he review the spiritual practice of "mystery (X-The Mystery)" from the Spirituality and Practice website.

Interestingly enough, the description on that website states, "Live with paradoxes. Give up the idea that you can always get it." The first reaction Alan had when taking the QFPI™— "I don't get it"— turned out to be the very thing he needed to work on.

People's initial reactions often gloss over an intuition, inkling, or deeper insight that lies below the surface. The QFPI™ allowed Alan to explore these insights, giving him access to more Acceptance and Presence in his life. He could relax the struggle and ultimately experience Flow while collaborating with others and creating a new set of practices. Indeed, through the help of a collaborator (actually, a real-life engineer) Alan now has a thriving creative project that was only a dream before.

Tricia: "From Coordinating Toward Potentiating"

In contrast to Alan, some people take the QFPI™ and, along with other tools provided in this collection, make more intentional efforts toward a positive journey of self-transformation.

> For reasons I still can't explain, I decided to invest in getting to know myself. In that moment, I shifted a set of beliefs about what I value and how willing I was to do the work to show up differently in my life. This QfP work and this space offered me a launchpad into my soul journey. It helped me name and explore aspects of my authentic self. This work propelled me into a whole new awareness of the mysterious workings of the universe, of which I am a part.

Tricia, the author of the above quote, was sharing about the journey she had taken over the previous six months. She first scored herself as Synthesizing/Coordinating with an A Score of 36 and a B Score of 42. Six months later, she had moved more toward Synthesizing with an A Score of 31 and a B Score of 34. This movement—in the direction of Potentiating—had occurred in part because she was opening up to working with cre-

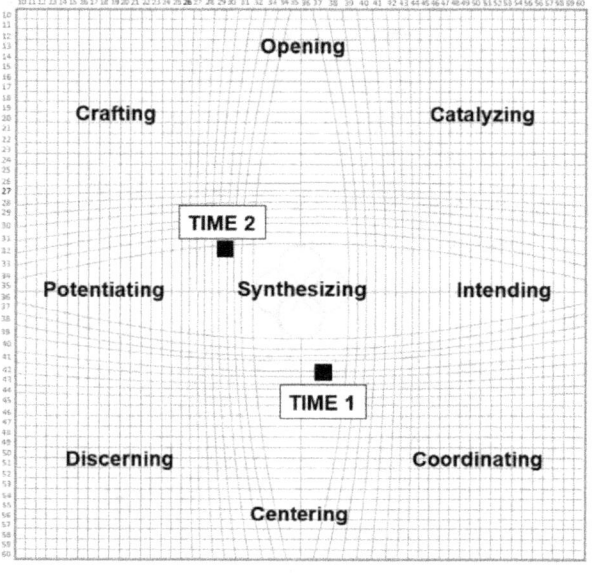

ative people and changes in her role as a mother. Tricia is both an editor and researcher, and her previous tendency had been to the more structured work in the province of Coordinating and Centering (she preferred the synonyms of Engineering and Organizing). Because of the COVID-19 pandemic, Tricia moved her workspace into her home. "I am more in tune with Nurturing Conditions than Engineering now, which I suppose makes sense with two kids at home engaged in virtual schooling," she shared. "I think, too, the movement up and across the grid can be attributed to an Opening that is happening within me." Reflecting further, she said,

> As a Synthesizer or Integrator in a time of extreme disconnect during the pandemic, I have struggled with not being able to engage the same communication pathways. I take on too many projects as a means of trying to maintain connections and end up highly distracted (and often overwhelmed) as a result of being pulled in too many directions.

By working with the feedback about Synthesizers, Tricia was able to focus on the strengths of the Attraction as a counterpoint to the cautions of distractibility.

> I am working toward a new way of showing up in the world. This has included gaining access to new knowledge communities and placing myself into (virtual) settings with new groups of people. I am starting to recognize the value of being a conduit of information and connectivity. As a "boundary spanner," I bring energy and attention to alternate perspectives in spaces where groupthink may otherwise occur. I tend to be a highlighter of themes when amid groups whose membership is more diverse. I love collecting data through conversations, emails, focus groups, or surveys—depending on what type of information is needed—and I bring an aptitude for using the tools to gather this information into the contexts where I function.

Clearly, Tricia had made decisions to stretch herself, and, along with her time spent with her children, this moved her into having more flexibility and experimentation. In many ways, her growth was away from fragmentation and toward wholeness. This is expressed in her comments about being more authentic and more connected to the universe.

Sarah: "From Handling to Helping People"

When taking the QFPI™, sometimes people get in touch with a deeper talent or calling. They realize that their current routines no longer fit this calling. Sarah is a nurse who had been struggling with incompetent management in her job when she first took the QFPI™. In the following five months, she had explored, she said, "deeper" parts of herself. She gradually realized that she could no longer tolerate the structures surrounding her career. When Sarah and I got back in touch, she was still in the same Attraction area as she was five months earlier, but she had moved slightly more toward Synthesizing. Specifically, her scores landed midway between Discerning (Negotiating) and Synthesizing (Integrating).

Many changes are happening in my life. A further change in management at work led me to resign. I am so happy to leave, as I have no more grace to put up with the unhealthy work culture. The feedback from the QFPI™ provided me with much perspective regarding my circumstances in the dysfunctional workplace. I realized that it was no longer a fit for a truer aspect of myself. The Negotiating and Discerning aspects showed me that I was learning to handle people better, which the difficult workplace required me to do. They, along with Synthesizing, helped me to realize that I could be very good at helping others (not just managing them).

Sarah reported that she "desired to honor these aspects of myself going forward in my life." She hoped to focus her energies more toward directly helping others. In tandem with this movement, Sarah decided to return to work as a holistic nurse and began studying depth psychology and Jungian dreamwork. She used the Attraction Matrix Commitment Statements from the beginning of the QFPI™ as milestones to report on her progress.

"Looking back, I realize that I have been committed to being more open to how my life is a process of being attracted to my essence," Sarah noted. "I had lost the grace to cope with what I could no longer tolerate, and this was not healthy self-care for me. I also have seen how my Attraction to different forces has worked to bring out my true potential."

Robert: "Sensing the Degree of Relatedness"

Other people who take the QFPI™ first see the feedback as validating what they already know to be true about themselves. They further use it to reflect on other areas of the map that they next want to explore. Robert's initial scores on the QFPI™ were A Score: 30 and B Score: 24. The results are shown in the graph below (see the "R" circle). Note that this chart uses different synonyms than previous charts shown in this section. In following up on changes since this first assessment, Robert shared the following:

Rather than retake the assessment, I read over the feedback pieces for each Attraction and sensed the degree of relatedness or lack thereof. I'm a holistic health coach, which is listed as a career embodiment for Nurturing. I absolutely love the way I'm able to serve, the active potentials always present, and my gifts that allow me to excel at it. For Nurturing [Potentiating] and Integrating [Synthesizing], I'd say 90 percent of that feedback applied to me, whereas Innovating [Opening] felt like 100 percent.

Instead of relying on the feedback from his single score, Robert took time to explore other Attractions. He wanted to discern what best fit his current life situation. He also indicated that he was definitively not attracted to any of the other areas, except for Challenging [Catalyzing], depicted as an arrow with a question mark on the grid. Reviewing the description related to this Attraction, Robert recognized that in the six months since he last experienced the QFPI™, he had some desire percolating for Catalyzing. "I affirmed and leaned into my profession in healthcare with greater certainty," he said. "I also noticed a growing affinity for start-ups and my lifelong ability to quickly identify risks in any personal or business endeavors." It helped his confidence to see that he was challenging himself more, bringing out more of his true self.

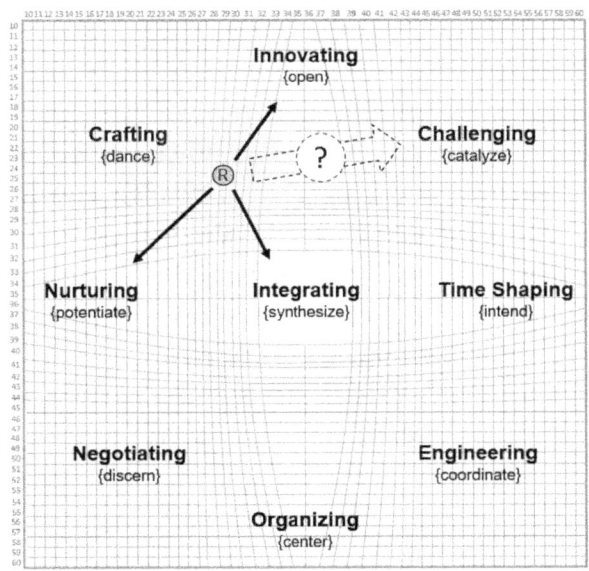

More Examples of Change

The above examples show just some possible ways of working with the QFPI™ Attraction Matrix. Some people stay in the same quadrant or area but notice subtle yet important changes. Others move back-and-forth from one quadrant to another. Over a few months, Trina moved from a solid Negotiating (Discerning), A Score: 27; B Score: 47 up toward Innovating (Opening), A Score: 31; B Score: 26. Her work responsibilities had increased, she was learning new skills working on a master's thesis, and changes were occurring at home. This required her to be more creative. Other people actually feel "stuck" with no movement. Usually, these are people who do not take the time to further explore the Attraction Matrix (meaning life's possibilities, future potential selves). However, even when we feel stuck, we may still be changing in considerable ways. In other words, we may be incubating a new Attraction.

One consultant was very upset about the climate of political polarization and racial injustice in the United States. He had enjoyed how the course helped him "contemplate the process of change, death, rebirth, and healing." He explained that these contemplations were not top-of-mind as he was depressed and agitated about the continued negative direction of society. "These events have been overwhelming and traumatizing. I've not experienced anywhere close to the resilience I thought or felt that I had." In reality, he had changed quite a bit. His original scores showed a balance between Innovating and Crafting (A Score: 24; B Score: 29), and he moved to the lower right toward Synthesizing and Coordinating (A Score: 38; B Score: 41). It appeared that he was moving more inward and gathering the perspective of the Engineer to make sense of what was going on. Over time (usually months), he appeared to vacillate between these two sectors of the matrix—being creative, then integrating, and then grounding before getting creative again. His Attraction was actually to cycle across time.

Others use the matrix more deliberately. One individual working in training and development in a company reported that the framework of the matrix "adds to my ability to be the Observer of myself. I notice how I am and am not being present in my life and with others." The distractibility of her primary attraction of "Synthesizing self" was taking away from her self-care. Accordingly, she reported moving more toward Crafting and Innovating to bring more self-care into her life as a way of being present.

Discussion

I hope that your own "time-empowerment" and "self-leadership" are two key takeaways that you glean from reading these brief case studies. In most examples, the person gained perspective on where they were in the longer time frame of their life trajectory. They walked away with some sense of empowerment. They owned their journey. Also, each person approached the exercise in their own authentic way. Alan took the time to specify his particular response to individual items and how he felt about them. Tricia took the feedback form information to heart and was able to apply specific insights from it to advance her own journey. Sarah used the commitment statements as milestones for looking backward and forward and setting new goals for herself. And Robert set the questionnaire aside entirely to explore what feedback resonated with him the most and discover what he might be attracted to next.

Robert used the QFPI™ feedback forms as a resource for contemplation. This speaks to the next chapter. Having worked with this tool for many years, I have realized that I, too, have either worked within or related to the world and other people from each of the Nine Attractions at some point. Clearly, I am not an Integrator and always prefer the creative energy that comes from Nurturing Conditions and Chaos. At the same time, situations and changes call on different aspects or features of my personality: strengths, talents, coping skills, resilience. I always return to Crafting. In this way, each of us can be an Integrator no matter where we are in the Attraction Matrix. We are all required, called, or otherwise *attracted* to move around, if only for brief moments, as the situation, our karma, and this happening life engages us.

Contemplation (QfP 3-4): Plan, Act, Repeat

You are asked to complete the QFPI™ on at least two occasions, ideally six months apart. After six months, come back to this chapter and answer the following questions.

1. Did you retake the QFPI™? Did it matter whether you did? Can you just look at the items, like Alan did? What do you notice if you take that approach?

2. What is your reflection—looking back—telling you about your journey through time?

    a. Do you feel the same or different about your path or trajectory?

    b. Do you feel more or less empowered in your orientation toward time?

    c. Does your life make more or less sense now?

    d. What has emerged about your sense of purpose or meaning?

3. How much change has occurred in your scores? Why?

    a. Were changes in your scores subtle? If so, were they still significant?

    b. Were changes in your scores dramatic (for example, jumping quadrants)? If so, were they not surprising or inconsequential?

4. Which of the following adjectives best describe your journey since the last time you took the QFPI™?

Stuck, Liberating, Germinating, Waiting, Pausing, Stopping, Opening, Reverting, Advancing, Retreating, Revealing, Hiding, Hunkering, Blasting, Fermenting, Decomposing, Vanishing, Nurturing, Negotiating, Unifying, Synthesizing, Befriending, Holding, Covering, Yearning, Clarifying, Mystifying

CHAPTER 5

Work and Play in the Attraction Matrix

An Ode to Practice

frying vegetables, browsing the internet, asking
   coworkers to do their job, figuring out an
   answer, meditating, listening for a friend,
   creating a new survey, watching the ocean

Each, its own color on the canvas

Yes
It takes practice
To let the paint dry
And watch the mandala emerge

~J.B.

On any given day, you may be called—or situations will engage you—to "practice" one or more of the Attractions, perhaps several at the same time. As the previous two chapters explained, you may have an overriding or typical tendency to live in a particular sector of the Attraction Matrix. At the same time, all sectors are available to us through work and play. Your ability to see every Attraction as an accessible part of your own life allows you to take the perspective of others, even if you rarely visit that area.

The Attractions also are daily opportunities for living well, for feeling whole and present to this happening life. You can view the Attractions as practices that can be performed with lesser or greater degrees of soulfulness. The first law of thermodynamics states that energy cannot be created or destroyed. In our human lives, this means that on any given day, we have only so much energy to spare, use, play with, and transform. The fact that we are given this energy is itself a call to practice. How will you use that energy? Will you use it to cultivate the Soulful Capacities, or will you use it to reinforce your ego?

Examples from My Own Practice

Daily practice, or time set aside for a specific purpose, is another aspect of our lives. Many spiritual paths require a daily practice: meditation, prayer, devotionals, worship, as well as service, charity, giving, and good deeds. These paths encourage us to not just "set time aside" but to weave the spirit of prayer, mindfulness, attentiveness, and goodwill into all our routines and daily activities. Below, I share how the Attractions manifest as a practice in my own life, even though I don't do these with prayerfulness or mindfulness. Indeed, as I show below, these practices are not perfect. They are just part of life.

In the movie *Groundhog Day*, the main character wakes up each day to repeat the same routines over and over in an endless and dreary cycle. This becomes so intolerable that the character ends up committing suicide—over and over. Gradually, he realizes that the problem is his own negativity, a poor attitude toward other people and his life. Slowly, every situation he encounters becomes an opportunity for being of service, offering charity, giving, or doing good deeds. Love is the primary motivation for his transformation. He breaks the cycle of suffering only when he fully realizes the potential of his own goodness.

In a similar way, we have the opportunity every day to practice each and every one of the Attractions. We can do so with Acceptance, Presence, Flow, and Synchronicity or with resistance, mindlessness, or awkwardness. I hope the examples I provide below help you see how common these opportunities are. Here are the ways in which my personality and ego navigate the Attractions with varying degrees of perfection, quality, and success. I begin each paragraph with the main signifier but also add key synonyms.

Opening/Innovating (to open; create; diverge). I am a vegetarian and like to cook; I enjoy seasoning rice dishes. In my press to be uniquely creative, I rarely get the flavor just right. My father, who spent much of his career in the food and restaurant business, would complain that my food had no "tam." In Thai cooking, *tam* means pounded food, which conveyed to me that flavors had to have some salt, pungency, and richness. I would follow recipes that started with frying a mixture of diced onion, garlic, and celery to create a "base" flavor and add salt, pepper, and other spices. Despite my need to innovate and create my own "special" seasoning blend, mastery has not yet taken hold. Just recently, I was experimenting again, and it did not work. My wife, for probably the fiftieth time in our twenty-five years of marriage, said, "Just add in some sugar and a splash of tamari." I said, "No, you can do that to your own dish." Of course, I tasted hers and, for the fiftieth time, changed my seasoning. From my ego standpoint, this did not seem like innovating. However, by diverging from "my way" and being in the Flow, I was able to enjoy "our" meal so much more.

Catalyzing/Challenging (to catalyze; take a risk; disrupt). I use social media (Twitter, Facebook, LinkedIn). Anyone who is familiar with these outlets knows they are filled with provocations and mindless chatter. I fail to see why people take all this virtual, electronic, fleeting communication so seriously. I think, "It is only a bunch of electronic bits of data that show up on a glass screen." I recently felt a need to challenge or disrupt all this seriousness and play the trickster. Facebook gives its users the opportunity by changing where one lives ("places lived"—"add city"). Over the past few months, out of a desire to disrupt how I am seen, I have changed where I live from San Antonio, Texas, to Ho Chi Minh City (Vietnam), to Dubrovnik (Croatia), to Copenhagen (Denmark), and Poggibonsi (Italy). At first, people would congratulate me on my move, not seeing that I was just playing around. I explained that I was taking a virtual tour around the world. Judging from the reactions I've seen (or failed to see), my Facebook friends pretty much just ignored me. From my ego standpoint, I was challenging (a playful "I'll show them"). As it turns out, many people also use social media for the fun of it. Perhaps I should stop trying to get attention and just accept Facebook for what it is.

Intending/Time Shaping (to intend; drive; motivate; activate; inspire). I am an entrepreneur. I run a business. As with any business, to stay successful, taking action is necessary. Ideally, this comes from having a vision, a mission, a plan, and, subsequently, using project management and other tools to ensure that the plan is carried out, customers are satisfied, and money comes in. It also means that I have to somehow motivate others to do their jobs. Recently, I have been working with interns who spent an entire summer helping out with various tasks. Just as they were getting up to speed (and doing quite well), the school season started. This was also the first time that school was in session during the COVID-19 pandemic. The students were subject to a whole new format for virtual learning. Suddenly, all the skills I helped them develop were not as available to the business—to "me"—as I had wanted. Of course, out of my own frustration, I judged them, the school system, and their teachers for needlessly piling on work that got in the way of my "all-important" business. From my ego standpoint, I had been on a steady path of Time Shaping, building layers of effectiveness and efficiency by training and cultivating talent. I had to apologize to the interns because of my occasional snarky and sarcastic comments. As often happens with Time Shaping, things don't turn out exactly the way we plan. Maybe I could do a better job of going with the Flow.

Coordinating/Engineering (to coordinate; calculate; calibrate). As part of my work, I schedule classes for students to attend. To make this work, we need a minimum number of students. Recently, a group of potential students from diverse agencies expressed interest. To determine if I had the minimum and that everyone could attend at the same time, I created an online survey that asked how many students would come and provided a list of about twelve potential dates and times. When the data came back from several agencies, it was clear that there was only one time slot that would work. I sent that information to everyone to confirm their attendance. In the meantime, others expressed interest. While still waiting for everyone to send their confirmation, I decided to just "put a flag in the sand" and set everything up for a time that seemed to work best. From my ego standpoint, I anticipated the need to coordinate diverse schedules by using email, surveys, and calendar tools. These are the province of the Coordinator or Engineer. From the viewpoint of Attraction, the forces of Form and Time Shaping synchronized together and evoked the appropriate action.

Centering/Organizing (to center; stabilize; ground). I make efforts every day to meditate. Every meditation teacher I know encourages people to pick a particular time of the day for routine meditation. This has worked only to some degree with me. Right now, as I write this, I am on vacation and have no specific schedule to adhere to. No plans. No demands. So even now, I could set up some schedule and stick to it. But that does not happen. I don't even try. What I have noticed, however, is that in spite of this randomness, there are times—sometimes for many days and even a few weeks—where I automatically wake up at the same time every morning, usually between 3:00 a.m. and 4:00 a.m. I just go to my meditation place and sit. There is no thought or plan I am aware of. It just happens. Something else is centering me. From my ego standpoint, I judge myself for not having discipline. From the viewpoint of Attraction, the force of Form sort of kicks me in the spiritual butt. It is no accident that it occurs so early in the morning. Many paths claim that the hours before dawn are the "time of the elixir," "time of ambrosia," or "the magic hours" that are the best for communing with spirit, God, the universe.

Discerning/Negotiating (to discern; communicate; use diplomacy). I was recently approached by a friend who does a form of meditation coaching. The approach requires completing a self-assessment to identify the best form of meditation. My friend then customizes the meditation for the client. We met. She gave me my assignment. It was very helpful. But then, someone reached out to me after being diagnosed with brain problems caused by COVID-19. Experiencing much mental fog, she could not concentrate. I met with my coach again and diplomatically shared that, because I already had a practice, my "COVID friend" would benefit more than me, and I requested my meditation coach use my payment to help. My coach friend and I then had a wonderful conversation about meditation. Her open-ended and caring questions allowed me to see the benefits of her proposed methods as well as other methods, and she also understood more about my own practice. It was very fulfilling because it did not result in any needed action. It was just a friendly meeting, with real listening and understanding. From my ego standpoint, I went into the conversation with some anxiety about alienating my coach friend. From the viewpoint of Attraction, we spent time discerning together and—just in being with that—found uplifting moments of intimacy. It was greatly satisfying to hear my coach friend say, "The timing is not right, right now" in a voice of complete Acceptance.

Potentiating/Nurturing (to bring out the potential; cultivate; facilitate; find a frame or context). About a week before Daylight Savings Time ended in the autumn, I had the idea of walking my six-year-old granddaughter to school the next morning. I live close enough that I can quickly make it happen to pick her up at 7:00 a.m. and take the beautiful twenty-minute walk, much of it along tree-lined paths and nearby meadows. At the same time, I learned from her parents that some child in the other granddaughter's school had just been diagnosed with the COVID-19 virus, and all children should stay home and consider quarantining. I waited a few days for the message that it was clear to go to school. Because of the change in time, the sun was up early, so we would not be in the dark while walking. Also, the virus had subsided. Somehow, while waiting, I noticed that the conditions were aligning for my potential idea to get realized. I was not frustrated about it. I just kept holding the intention. From my ego standpoint, I saw the potential of having a nice time with my granddaughter. However, conditions had to fall into place; the timing had to be right. We walked together for about four or five days before she got bored or something else came up.

Crafting/Dancing (**to dance** [with energy, **with the situation**]; **design; customize**). This is where I spend most of my time or, better, where time enfolds its gifts into my personality. I think it is best to say no more and let these writings speak for themselves.

Synthesizing/Integrating (**to synthesize; unify**). Recently, my colleagues and I were preparing a final report analyzing several months of work done for a client. Some team members summarized statistical data, while others synthesized themes from interviews. My job was to design the final recommendations based on these data. I had been involved at every step along the way and had developed most of the recommendations. One coworker suggested changes to recommendations that I had already made. These were helpful, but I needed to see data to support these changes. We met and talked it through. As a result, some important insights were added that I would not have thought of on my own. From my ego standpoint, these new ideas revealed a "glitch" in my synthesis. But in reality, the energy of the Integrating Attraction was working as it should. This project required the many hours spent by all team members and an additional layer of perspective. The feedback for this Attraction states, "Seeing the pattern and helping others to see it as well." In this case, someone else was helping me see the pattern, and it had nothing to do with either of our egos.

Contemplation (QfP 3-5): Your Life as a Canvas

*"Life is a great big canvas, and you should
throw all the paint on it you can."*

~DANNY KAYE, AMERICAN ACTOR, SINGER, DANCER,
COMEDIAN, MUSICIAN, AND PHILANTHROPIST

This exercise has two parts. Just notice what comes up as you do this.

PART 1. First, reflect on your day. How much time did you spend in any of the nine Attraction areas? For purposes of the exercise, assume that outside of sleep and other times when you are conserving energy, you have only sixteen hours of time to use: thirty-two half-hour segments—thirty-two buckets. Also, because you only have so much energy to spare, you cannot spend more than twelve of those segments in any one of the nine Attractions. Realize that the grid below has 108 "time buckets," and you can fill in only thirty-two.

Color or mark in the boxes within the half-hour block that you **spent most of that time** in the Attraction. Also, note the time of the day. It is possible that there was one part of your day (late morning, early evening) with two or more Attractions going on at once.

	Morning		Afternoon		Evening	
	Early	Late	Early	Late	Early	Late
Opening to life; attracted to essence; letting go; playing, enjoyment; allowing yourself to get distracted; immersed in an activity						
Potentiating self and others; helping; serving; bringing something to fruition; participating in the cultivation of care, community, teamwork						
Centering through organization, routines, regular activities, meditation or other practice, grounding, returning from distraction						
Crafting and dancing through designing, customizing, tailoring, co-creating, playing with tools or any media						
Discerning and negotiating with others; listening, empathizing, finding common ground, mediating, relating in heedful ways						
Catalyzing or challenging, taking a risk or a stand, using a critical eye, not settling for some rule or norm, going against it						
Intending or scheduling, planning, following up and implementing those plans, getting things done, accomplishment						
Coordinating or engineering your day or week; coordinating elements, activities, people, things; calculating what needs to be done						
Synthesizing or integrating any or all of the above; making sense of it all; giving it meaning and purpose; finding balance						

PART 2. Reflect on the earlier quote from Danny Kaye. As you review the pattern above, ask yourself if you are using the entire canvas of your life. What will you do differently tomorrow?

CHAPTER 6

Relationships

An Ode to Neighbors

You were astonished how,
every now and then,
you would pivot your head to the left
or look for a moment to the right

Someone else was walking there,
swimming, hiking, gazing up into the miracle
    starlight, or
just having a bad day

Just a slight glance
and another path appears
For them too
It seemed

Either way
You asked them
To get your head out of
your way

~J.B.

The idea of "attraction" is most often applied in common language when we refer to a "sexual" desire. Outside of sexuality, we feel drawn to certain people and find some more attractive in their personalities than others. It is in and through our relationships with others that many people learn about the Level 2 Attraction toward the cosmological forces. These forces work in our lives through how and when—in the unfolding journey—we are drawn to work, live, and love other people.

I have not yet done any systematic research with the QFPI™, which some may criticize. This is especially the case regarding how the Attractions play out in relationships. However, I do have some personal experiences to draw from. Because of my Crafting tendency, how I describe these experiences likely will be colored by my own bias. The examples below may encourage you to reflect on how you work with others in your life who may have a different or similar Attraction.

My Organizing Coworker

One of my coworkers had been employed with me for about five years. She had taken the QFPI™ on several occasions across that time. Each time she landed in the Organizing Attraction, and she reported that the information in the feedback form fit her very well. This was not a surprise to either of us. She mostly performed in the role of project management and organized files, worked closely with consultants on their own tasks and timelines, and kept me updated on a regular basis. During our time together, we both noticed gradual changes in both our matrices.

I should point out that we were, more or less, working very closely together on projects. She was highly intelligent (emotionally and intellectually) and was learning and growing at a fast rate. I asked her to step up and engage in more business development because we were working on commercializing some new software. This meant that she had to see the world somewhat more from my lens as an inventor. I complemented her efforts by assisting with her project-management demands. As the chart shows, we moved slightly closer to each other's Attraction over time. While many other things were happening in my life, this was a period of strong business development. I attributed much of this movement toward Form and Organizing, as seen in the chart, to both the relationship and the business.

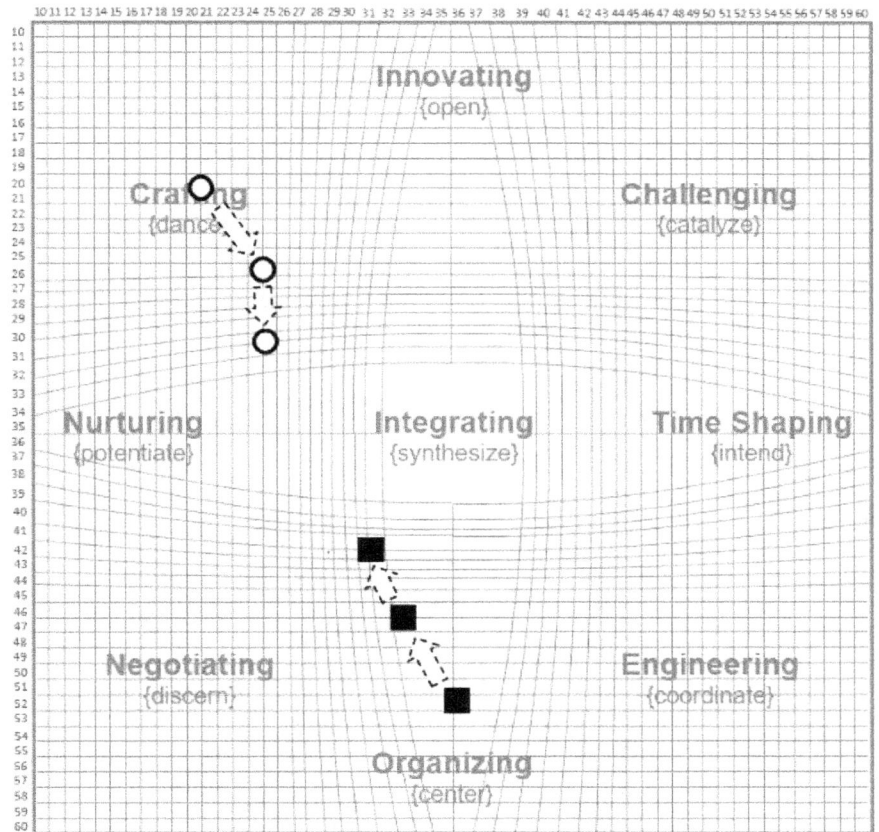

My Marriage

From time to time in this collection, I share stories from my marriage in the Reflections contained within chapters. Over the past fifteen years, I have asked my wife to take the QFPI™. As I have shared, I tend to stay in the upper-left quadrant, but I do move around a bit. My wife, on the other hand, consistently scores pretty much the same on every occasion. Her score is always just south of Synthesizing. She is a self-avowed Integrator. Her score is always centralized toward Organizing, not toward other Attractions. Despite this fact, she does not see herself attracted to Organizing, per se. Instead, she believes she can take the perspective of all the other Attractions. In fact, she does this in her work as a psychotherapist and sees this as a developed talent.

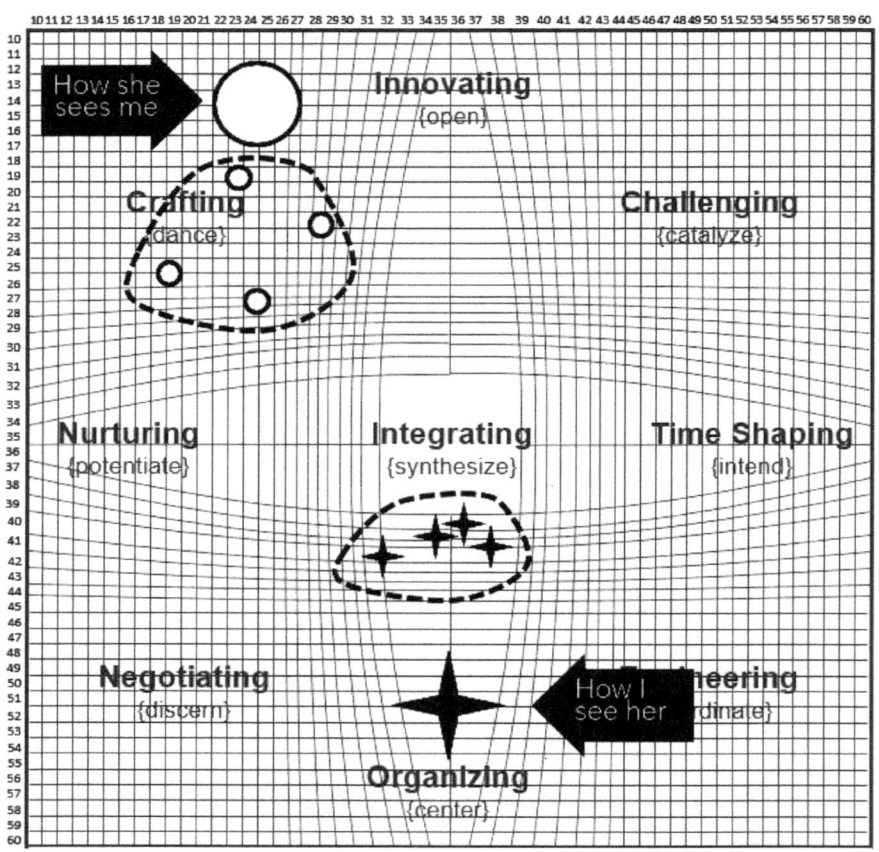

This is, of course, her perspective. My perspective—my bias—is somewhat different. Similarly, she sees me a certain way as well. Below is an example of our different scores across time. These are shown as shapes within the dotted line areas. I am represented as the circle, and she is represented by the stars. What I am about to share may come across as a diagnosis of great incompatibility in my marriage. However, there is also the idea that "opposites attract" and stay together. The key word in that last sentence, if you have been paying attention, is "attract."

First, my scores tend to exhibit more range and diversity than her scores (that is, the dotted line around my circles is wider than the line around her stars). My wife uses certain adjectives to describe me, including "wild," "random," and "creative," and believes that I am woefully lacking in organizational skills. Her perception of me is represented by the large circle in the upper-left quadrant. In other words, across time, she has averaged her perception into a general impression that: (a) does not take into account the variation, and (b) sees me as a more extreme version of myself. Frankly, I have done the same with her. I do not see her as an Integrator as much as an Organizer. This, of course, has something to do with our different ways of doing things in running the household. You can imagine that I am not a big fan of routines and household chores (dishes, garbage, cleaning).

A number of insights comes from this example that aligns with research on communication and functioning in marriages but applies more broadly. First, people have a tendency to "type" others, and this may be a function of their own Attractions. I see my wife as more of an Organizer than she actually is, and she sees me as more of a Crafter and Innovator than I actually am. This is one reason why I avoid referring to the Attractions as types. The use of "types" leaves too much room for projection and seeing others as more static or stable than dynamic and changeable. As I hope to have shown in the preceding chapters, many subtle but significant changes can occur in our quest for presence. Either way, there is a *contrast effect* and a *halo effect* in social perception. We do project. We see others who have Attraction tendencies that are opposite from us as contrasting with our tendencies, so we pay less attention to subtle differences. We also clump these differences together as a "halo" in a sort of, "If you have seen one Organizer, you have seen them all."

Second, we have an opportunity to learn from others. We can utilize their perspective as a set of strengths to enhance our own journey. In the case of my coworker described above, I was able to see how I could adopt a different approach as the business required. In the case of my wife, she has a very calming and centering effect on me, especially when I struggle, feel that no one understands, and get overwhelmed. I have learned a great deal about the force or law of Form because of my marriage and in ways that I feel that I could not have done otherwise. This is why I advocate that you have others in your life complete the QFPI™ across time along with you. Again, we are on the path of this happening life, and we can always help each other see things in a new light.

My Creative Colleagues

Over the past ten years, I have worked off and on with another colleague who hangs out a lot in the Innovator area. She explores new ideas and technologies and has diverse interests in areas we share in common. For a period of several years, I had hired her and her team as consultants to help us develop our website. We actually developed about five websites. We would meet, come up with new ideas together, she would say, "That is a great idea, let's do it!"—and we were off and running. It was exciting, fun, and played directly into the Attraction we both had to the creative energies represented by the force of Chaos.

Having someone who is close to your own Attraction but in a different vector can be like finding a spiritual friend or "QfP partner." While no one is exactly like you, these "Attraction neighbors" can help you tap into the energies of the Attraction in a new way because they speak a similar language. This is where the experience of Flow can be cultivated with great depth (see *QfP Book 2*). Conversations are easy. Ideas come fluently. And it all just seems like the right next step to take.

I know others with a similar innovative Attraction, and the energy when we get together is amazing. There is a real, palpable Attraction. This felt emotional and somatic sense of Attraction is, I believe, the Radiant Forces speaking to us through other people. When we pay attention to the tone, quality, and vibration of the Attraction, we notice important differences. My Attraction to my coworker and the growing business helped me to move more toward Centering. My Attraction to my wife helped me to have more Routine and required me to navigate life transitions from one Form to another (see *QfP Book 4*). My Attraction to my colleague gave me more energy for creativity, fun, and play.

Contemplation (QfP 3-6): The Other

You are asked to share your QFPI™ insights with others and for them to do the same by sharing with you. The contemplation here is straightforward. Just share your answers to the following questions.

✦ What do you have in common?

✦ What are your differences?

✦ What can you share with each other about your insights from the three previous contemplations?

- Contemplation (QfP 3-3): Gaze at Your Map, Study It, Revise It
- Contemplation (QfP 3-4): Plan, Act, Repeat
- Contemplation (QfP 3-5): Your Life as a Canvas

CHAPTER 7

An Attraction to a Path

Ode to Dread

Spiky spokes have many wheels
Vacant arms, their many spiral galaxies.
From that first dreaded step, you moved away
Or in, perhaps.

And then, in the breadth of a
heartbeat,
You were on your knees:
Grateful for that terror
That sent you looking.

How was it that you were
Pulled,
With all those others:
Spinning,
Traveling,
Spokes, into the
Arms of Wonder?

~J.B.

The journey I am about to describe represents an Attraction toward life and away from the anxiety of *having* to show up to life. On the surface, it will appear that my Attraction occurred in the intellectual domain of life. My hope is that you will look below the surface. I hope you can see a deeper connection to your own life and how your own journey about showing up to life has been. To help see this connection, I list a few of my own personal beliefs (inklings or insights) after each segment below.

Anxiety: Origins of the Quest for Presence Inventory™

Around the time of my parents' divorce when I was eleven, I started waking up in the morning with an aching pit in my chest and stomach, a deep yearning for something. It took me a few years to find the "anxiety" label for my feelings. I did not know what was happening. I could not determine any cause for this, not a single dream, type of dream, or even a particular set of thoughts. It was a free-floating sensation without any mental content. Usually, after about five to ten minutes, the sensation would subside. These morning anxiety episodes would come and go, but they occurred several times a week. They lasted for years, only gradually diminishing in my thirties.

I mostly kept this to myself, like any eleven-year-old who had no clue what was happening with "growing up" feelings. I mentioned it to my mother and grandmother. They were of little help, being preoccupied with picking up the pieces of my family. I suspected then that it had something to do with the divorce—my experience of the force of Chaos brought about by my parents' disintegrating marriage, the drama, the fights, and the alcohol. I also was not comfortable talking to my dad about it. I learned much later about the phenomena of *adult children of alcoholics* and *adult children of divorce*. I also learned about *separation anxiety*, in which children show clinginess and distress while anticipating separation from loved ones. Meeting others with similar adult-child experiences and family problems with alcohol has been an essential part of my path toward healing.

I did not fully evaluate this morning anxiety until my junior year in college, but I did find a way to short-circuit it. When I was sixteen, I worked at a summer camp in upstate New York. Every morning, someone would crank up the record player and place the microphone next to the all-campus loudspeakers for the morning wake-up music. As the summer progressed, I requested to do these honors, which required getting up before everyone and walking from my cabin on the outskirts of campus. So, for many mornings I played "Rockin' Robin" by Michael Jackson. In anticipation of this single act, I felt an exuberance and vitality that replaced any anxiety. Morning music has been a balm ever since.

In college, I had to write a term paper for an interdisciplinary class in my first semester as a freshman at the State University of New York (SUNY) at Purchase (1972). This "cluster" course was titled "Women," and it was taught by three women: author and feminist historian Bell Gale Chevigny; physicist, author, and feminist Evelyn Fox Keller; and anthropologist Judith Friedlander. This was the first of a series of life-changing encounters with teachers, mentors, and guides who helped me heal my anxiety.

My paper was on the relationship between feminist writer Simone de Beauvoir (author of *The Second Sex* and more than twenty other books) and her lifelong partner, existentialist philosopher Jean-Paul Sartre (author of *No Exit* and *Being and Nothingness*, among many other works). I had read *No Exit* in high school and was fascinated by the fact that de Beauvoir and Sartre had a nonexclusive sexual relationship for more than fifty years, they deeply supported and read each other's works, and so much of their lives were "out in the open." They were not hidden, like what I felt were the shadows of my own family. And my anxiety lurked in those shadows.

KEY INSIGHT

Find positive role-models, a place where you belong, where you can keep learning and uplift and be uplifted by others.

✤ Many people have "adverse childhood experiences" (ACEs). Trauma, violence, and physical or sexual abuse are especially difficult and can have long-term impacts on health. Fortunately, we all have the ability to transform stress into a positive resource and achieve positive adaptation, post-traumatic growth, and a positive redefinition of the self. We can lessen and even eradicate negative long-term effects of ACEs.

✤ How does this happen? For me, discovering positive role-models in healthy adult relationships was the beginning. I met with and learned from others who struggled with parents who either divorced or suffered from alcoholism. I found someplace I belonged. I kept learning. I found ways to do something for the community. I played uplifting music.

Discovering Essence

About my first year of high school, I was just browsing in the public library and discovered a section on different religions. I did a book report on the Hindu scripture, the Bhagavad Gita, which talked about ignorance (*avidya*) as one becoming attached to anything other than one's soul. I began to suspect that my anxiety was born out of attachment and ignorance. The path from ignorance was meditation and finding a teacher, a guru. So, I learned and practiced meditation from a guru, a teacher from India. I continued to study philosophy. All of this was quite exciting, and my young mind was soaking it all up. But I still felt disorganized, ungrounded, and distracted.

About this time, a friend suggested I read *The Center of the Cyclone: An Autobiography of Inner Space* by John C. Lilly. Lilly described a comprehensive methodology for getting more in touch with one's essence. He shared advice from a medical school teacher who had pointed him to J. B. S. Haldane's dictum: "You will not understand what is necessary in the way of scientific control unless you are the first subject in your experiments." Another friend bought me a copy of *The One Quest* by Claudio Naranjo, who described different approaches to psychological and spiritual development.

A common theme in both books was the distinction between one's ego and one's more essential self, or "essence." The purpose of any spiritual path is to help seekers understand this distinction and live more from the essence (or higher self, transcendent witness, inner guardian). Lilly described different "ego fixations" or "ego deviations" he learned from Óscar Ichazo and the Arica School. The work and practices of the Arica school were designed to reduce the ego so we can experience cosmic energy and love:

> As long as one holds onto the beliefs in the ego, as opposed to the beliefs in the Essence, one is in the service of self-destruction; one is under the dominance of phobic forces, of the true paranoia of being persecuted and prosecuted by the cosmic forces (Lilly, 1972).

Naranjo, who also studied with Ichazo, made the distinction between the neurotic personality and that of a healthy person, the latter having more of a sense of being present to life and the choices one makes. Naranjo quotes from the psychoanalyst Helmuth Kaiser. "The rifts in the neurotic's personality did not permit him to be 'present' to the same degree in his actions and words as are healthier personalities" (Naranjo, 1972). Naranjo went on to explain how the neurotic is a victim who feels he has no choice and whose words and actions are not truly his own.

When I discovered that both Naranjo and Lilly had studied with Ichazo and the Arica School, I had to learn more. In addition to my morning anxiety, I started having experiences where, in the transition from sleep to waking, I struggled with a sense of being frozen or stuck. I would have to pound my fists to wake up. I grew more scared than anxious. The meditation I had learned was not helping me. Indeed, because of this new experience of being frozen, I feared that meditation was making things worse.

With the financial help of my grandmother, I signed up for the forty-day Arica training at Lyndon State College in Barre, Vermont. I read that the training focused equally on body awareness practices (yoga, bioenergetics, self-massage), heart-centered and emotional awareness techniques (chanting, group process work, heart meditations), and mental clarity and detachment from thought (various meditation practices).

KEY INSIGHT

Find a path that opens your heart.

❖ Throughout history, humanity has searched for answers to understand and embrace: the spiritual dimension of life, life beyond death, and the reason we have consciousness. Most religions have some answers, and no single religion has all the answers.

❖ Why, then, do so many people maintain a dogmatic adherence to only one set of beliefs? In my case, my anxiety was so great that it forced me to remain open, refrain from imposing a belief system, and learn as much as I could from diverse religions and spiritual paths. I discovered that all of us have a beautiful essence that transcends any one path. And the more I paid attention to my heart and essence (versus a belief system), the less anxiety I had.

The training consisted of a "three centers" approach to personal development, with diverse body, mind, and heart practices. As a nineteen-year-old, I was one of the youngest attendees. It was perhaps the most transformational time in my life. I learned many types of exercises for grounding my body and reducing my anxiety, some of which I still practice today, almost fifty years later. I met and learned from dozens of others who were also seeking personal growth. My morning anxiety reduced significantly yet did not fully vanish. However, I had found at least one path that could help.

The Enneagram

One aspect of this path was the Enneagram as developed by Ichazo and the Arica School. The Enneagram is a nine-point system for understanding and organizing many aspects of human experience and spiritual development. This was only one aspect of Arica, and there were 108 Enneagrams to help navigate different aspects of spiritual development. Of these, I understood the most important were the Enneagrams of the Holy Ideas and the Virtues. The "ego fixations" and personality types that Lilly and Naranjo had described were important to identify primarily because these were at the root of neurosis, suffering, addiction, and negative emotional states. In essence, the ego fixations were subjective (unconscious) aspects of personality that had separated from the pure objective and vibrant essence of our true being. As we emerge from childhood, we forget the holiness of the universe, the Holy Ideas, the "cosmic energies" that Lilly described. We grow less inclined to the more positive, objective, and conscious emotions of the virtues and more attached to subjective feelings, like anxiety.

An essential takeaway from my experience of Arica was that one does not learn about the ego or essence from books and self-assessments. We have to be completely and totally *present* to—not escape from—our anxiety. We have to bring our grounded body, open heart, and clear mind to the moment. Also, we can most objectively see our biases and ego-states only from the outside. We need other seekers who are willing to be completely and even brutally honest about our limitations. We best learn from a community that doesn't just talk about personality types but works on the essence.

KEY INSIGHT

Talk and learn with others who can share a map of awakening.

❖ As we grow and mature, we realize how each person has a different character, set of values, belief systems, as well as strengths and weaknesses. The more we pay attention to these differences with an open heart, the more we realize a certain spiritual beauty to the human condition and the shared suffering that is part of our common humanity.

❖ How can we see this beauty? For me, it helped to have other searchers around me who were vulnerable, willing to own that they were on a quest. It helped to have a map or a system we could share to explain these differences. The Enneagram was only the first map for me, and there are dozens of systems available.

Interdisciplinarity and Time

At the same time that I was discovering Arica, I was also growing in my intellectual curiosity. The interdisciplinary nature of the Women cluster at SUNY Purchase opened my eyes to the idea that knowledge lies in the border *between* and *across* disciplines rather than within any one discipline. At SUNY Purchase, I was offered the opportunity to "declare" my own interdisciplinary major, so I combined philosophy and psychology and labeled it *neurotheology*. My interest in the brain came from reading John Lilly's book. His research with consciousness, brains, and dolphins led Lilly to postulate that the brain functioned like a biocomputer. We could program our brains to create higher states of consciousness and reduce negative emotional states.

My two supporting professors for neurotheology were Robert Neville from philosophy and George Wolf from psychology. I worked in Dr. Wolf's lab cleaning rat cages and helping out with rat studies. I also took courses in philosophy with Robert Neville and Christine Grontkowski. One short semester, I took a course with Neville on

Sanskrit as a way to further study the Bhagavad Gita. I also took a course with Dr. Grontkowski and Dr. James Currin on the philosophical implications of quantum mechanics. It was in the course on quantum mechanics that I first learned about quantum field theory.

I learned that the atomic model of matter (the Bohr model), with a core nucleus surrounded by electrons that orbit the nucleus, was only an approximation of reality and was by then obsolete in modern science. I learned that the picture was closer to one of dense and diffuse clouds of particles and waves continually emitting energy. Basic particles were more like spherical clouds of probability. The main text for our class was Werner Heisenberg's *Physics and Philosophy*.

I learned three things from this course that have stayed with me all these years. First, there is no universal time clock; time is relative to the observer (*relativity*). Second, we can never know the present moment in its details (the *uncertainty principle*). Third, reality, or how those fields and clouds of atoms unfold in time, is to a great extent dependent on the position of the observer and the tools at hand (the *observer effect*). This idea that reality was fundamentally uncertain provided me—in a paradoxical way—with a sense of security, taking the edge off my uneasiness about the world.

KEY INSIGHT

*Find a topic or endeavor that excites you so much
that you want to keep on learning.*

Of course, in this (and later segments) of my journey, I focused more and more in the intellectual domain of growth. I discovered that I am a life-long learner, especially for science, big ideas, and interdisciplinary projects. But the main thing was about seeing and making connections. I made up for the lack of connection I felt as a child and the pain I felt. We never know what we might discover through these connections. For me, insight into the brain and the nature of time was so exciting that it kept me moving on past the pain.

My Introduction to the Modern Science of Psychology

Needless to say, I dove more into science. In my sophomore year at SUNY, I worked as a research assistant in the psychophysiology lab of Dr. Richard (Richie) Davidson. He and Dr. Clifford (Cliff) Saron became my close mentors—and friends, like big brothers—over the next few years. It was then that I shared my experience of morning anxiety with Richie. I remembered John Lilly's recounting of the dictum to take oneself as a subject in one's own experiment. Richie taught me how to develop a hypothesis, identify measures to test that hypothesis, and conduct my very first study of psychology.

Given my understanding of the neurotic personality, I hypothesized that morning anxiety might be more prevalent among those with neurotic tendencies. Richie introduced me to the Eysenck Personality Inventory (EPI), a brief psychological measure that assessed neuroticism (N) and extraversion-introversion (I-E). I asked about twenty students to complete the EPI along with a few questionnaire items asking how often they felt anxiety either upon waking or while trying to fall asleep. At that time, there were no computers, only desktop calculators. By hand, I manually entered the data and calculated correlations to assess if there was any relationship between N, I-E, and morning or evening anxiety. I discovered a positive correlation between extraversion and the tendency to have morning anxiety, but no relationship between anxiety and neuroticism in this sample of students.

In some ways, this was a relief. It was incorrect to apply this correlational finding back to myself. (Yes, I was one of the data points in the study.) Just because I had morning anxiety did not mean that I did *not* have tendencies toward neuroticism. However, I began to reflect on other ideas: namely that, upon waking, someone inclined to extraversion would begin to reflect on being with others and interacting in the world. The transition from sleep to waking may engage a sense of anticipation, and possibly dread, that was more pronounced for extraverts. (As a side note, the study of morning anxiety, childhood anxiety, and sleep cycles has grown considerably since 1976.)

KEY INSIGHT

*Our growth depends on not only enfolding factual information
(that comes from a book, from an occupation, or from
a field of study) but also enfolding information about
the heart (that comes from working alongside a teacher
or someone who cares enough about our growth).*

Finding a mentor, becoming an apprentice, and learning the details of a specific profession—these now seem essential for my growth. At some point, the actual content or body of knowledge within a profession became less important than finding someone who cared enough about my learning that they were willing to challenge me, push me harder, and not settle for excuses. I just had to study, do the work, learn the routines and the jargon.

The Brain Has a Personality

Being a lab assistant for Richie and Cliff meant studying psychophysiology, the relationship between measures of physiology and mental states and emotions. My undergraduate thesis assessed the relationship between self-induced emotional states and left-vs.-right brain EEG activation in both the frontal and parietal lobes. My hypothesis followed from the previous research literature I had compiled for Richie. That research suggested that negative emotions—like fear and anxiety—were experienced when the left hemisphere of the brain was more active than the right hemisphere.

I hypothesized that introspective *experience* of positive emotional states would be associated with relative left-frontal hemisphere activity, whereas the *experience* of negative states would correlate with relative right-frontal activity. This hypothesis was not supported. However, an interesting finding emerged. The results pointed to participants' *resting* EEG, not their *task-related* EEG while performing the introspection. Those who had relatively greater right-frontal activity while in the resting state (while doing nothing before, during, and after the experiment) were more likely to rate their emotions as more intense. I understood for the first time that some people feel their feelings more intensely regardless of the positive or negative valence of any particular emotion.

A significant number of studies have explored trait frontal EEG asymmetry as a possible index of personality, what Richie has called *affective style*. The takeaway from my thesis pertained to our internal life: how we look within and explore inner and deeper feelings, emotions, and images. Events in life stimulate, evoke, or trigger emotions. These come and go. Regardless of the valence of these emotions, there is something within us that leads us to fully embrace the richness of the experience, whatever it is.

Each of us has the ability to experience life deeply. Apparently, my affective style was to experience anxiety more deeply. Combined with the inner work I was doing through meditation and Arica exercises, I started to understand that I experience life more deeply than many others I knew. Anxiety was just part of the affective landscape. My undergraduate thesis—and my study of emotions—broadened my perspective further. The Uncertainty Principle suggested my anxiety may have a basis in recognizing the inherent uncertainty of reality. The EEG study suggested that we are each wired differently to a spectrum of depth in the experience of emotions.

KEY INSIGHT

Be prepared to find something new
every time your curiosity awakens.

A vast world resides within each of us. It contains more than thoughts and mental chatter. There is emotion and emotional depth and insights that emerge by patiently listening into this depth. It is extremely limiting to look at our brain as only having left and right sides. There is a deep brain, a surface brain, a forward and a back, and so much more. Our human experience of life is enormously rich and varied, so much so that no single human being will have every experience. Every day there is something new to behold.

Master's Thesis: Interdependence over Time

Richie and Cliff helped me navigate the transition to graduate school. I attended the University of Texas at Austin (UT-Austin), where I studied clinical, social, and personality psychology with coursework in organizational behavior and consulting. The social psychologist Jeffrey Berman graciously suggested and supervised my master's thesis on the relationship between love and power in romantic relationships. How I went from brain research to this topic is a long story. Suffice it to say that, as I alluded to above in my women's studies, I continued to feel anxiety and fear in my close relationships. The close-relationship attachment issues—and related anxiety—that led me to study de Beauvoir and Sarte and then emotions now led me to better understand relationships themselves.

I had also just met Rick Archer, another wonderful mentor at UT, who taught a graduate-level seminar on close relationships. After drawing data from the student population, my thesis examined 100 male-female couples at different stages of romantic relationships—from early dating to marriage for over ten years. Many insights came from that data, including the confirmation of the hypothesis that the person in a relationship who has greater feelings of love is also the one who tends to have less power in the relationship. Assessing each couple's relationship status one year after their first ratings, I found that couples were more likely to have broken up or divorced based on the power imbalance, regardless of the degree of love or love imbalance. This insight helped me understand my parents' situation. My childhood anxiety came from overexposure to conflict, intense fights, and my father's rage-a-holism. The power imbalance between my parents hurt my growth but also sent me searching for answers.

My thesis also yielded data that allowed me to look at time in relationships. Of greatest interest was the pattern of satisfaction and attachment among couples at different stages of their relationship. The data showed a tendency for flip-flopping attachment: When one partner reported more attachment, the other partner reported less. At the same time, partner satisfaction tended to rise and fall in tandem. I inferred an ongoing dance in relationships that needed to happen for couples to endure. There had to be a give-and-take. If both partners grew too attached at the same time—too enmeshed and absorbed—that was unhealthy. Conversely, if both felt less attached at the same time, the relationship would dissolve. My attention shifted from looking at individual differences in personality to seeing how time and relationships played a significant role in our experience of life.

KEY INSIGHT

Life, and the relationships we have with others, is made up of exquisite patterns that emerge and play out over time. If we wait and we listen, we can see and appreciate these patterns. It can be quite liberating.

Despite all of my intellectual learning, I stumbled and suffered greatly in my closest romantic relationships. I easily fell in love and grew over-attached, and my anxiety blossomed within the grips of jealousy. So, I used the strength of my intellect to better understand what I was lacking. Again, as in other segments of my journey, I discovered a pattern that lifted me beyond my own egoic self. This was a pattern that could only emerge in and through time. It was a great revelation for me to see that everything changes in a patterned way in close, personal relationships. This was a spiritual insight. I learned that intellectual insight does not guarantee spiritual growth.

A Return to Ego: Power and Influence over Time

My interest in conflict and the power side of the love-power equation continued. My dissertation advisor for my PhD was Janet Taylor Spence. At the time, Janet was president of the American Psychological Association, and I was always anxious to be around her intense intelligence and power. This kind of anxiety was much more grounded and manageable than the free-floating childhood remnants I have described above. Two things are poignant about Janet. First, she pioneered the development of measures of anxiety as a personality trait two years before I was born. Second, despite my fear of her, she was always warm-hearted, supportive, and friendly. For my dissertation, she helped me develop a personality measure from scratch. Using techniques from psychometrics and assessing hundreds of students in various studies, I was able to distinguish the need for power (for having one's way, asserting power through position) from the need for influence (able to impact others, persuade, or change them).

In a structured experiment, I observed students with these different needs interacting with others in a brief discussion task that required resolving a conflict. In particular, students' behavior was rated on how much they exhibited signs of tension (tightness in expression, anxiety). It became clear that power-oriented individuals were actually less sensitive to others' ideas and opinions, especially as the task was drawing to an end and a decision had to be made. Those with a stronger need for power, which was more ego driven (correlating with narcissism), clearly showed less of a tendency to care about the outcomes of the group and more about asserting themselves.

These studies showed that, depending on their motivation and the situation they face, people are not always present to each other. Those with a high need for power and influence are less present to changes in the social situation. This is relatively truer for men when they are in positions of leadership. It became clearer and clearer to me that the situation we are in—especially the degree of conflict we face and the degree of control we have—influences our level of anxiety.

I remembered that my childhood was filled with many situations where my parents fought with each other, and I remembered that I had no control over their behaviors. It made more and more sense that I would be anxious, and somehow this lessened my anxiety further. My anxiety was really not about my adult self. It came from memories of an earlier me.

KEY INSIGHT

Your behavior matters, and you have more behavioral choices when you can let go of your ego. With this freedom, more possible patterns will emerge over time on your journey, giving your life more breadth and depth.

✣ This segment of my life (my PhD dissertation) directly followed the previous segment (my Master's thesis). I kept wanting to observe and look for patterns over time and look deeper into what makes some temporal patterns emerge more than others. My doctoral training hammered into my brain the overarching belief that *all human behavior is a function of nature and nurture, genetics and upbringing (learning and memory), and—in day-to-day life—our personality and the situations we find ourselves in.*

✣ How much, then, is really under control? Where does the self come in? How much can we control our destiny? I began to see the answers to those questions in the actual behavior of participants in the experiment. Those with less pressure to meet their ego (power) needs were more flexible in their behavior and less tense. Again, going back to my first insights about ego versus essence, a certain freedom comes when we don't have to only get what we only want.

Temporal Context

The thesis and the dissertation taught me the importance of temporal context. As a young scientist, I realized that the power of observation brought the ability to see things that would not ordinarily be observable. And these patterns of behavior over time were the most fascinating. I used the analogy of taking a snapshot of a swarm of birds, a murmuration, where hundreds of birds swim and whirl together and apart in an ever-changing pattern, a continual *folding* and *unfolding*. A single snapshot could not do justice to the beauty, nuance, and exquisite detail of the actual event. Even a string of snapshots—digital sections—could not convey the *context* of the real phenomena. Most importantly, there is an inherent *wholeness-in-time* to the murmuration, a wholeness that can be studied in and of itself.

This was such a powerful epiphany for me that I wrote a paper synthesizing eighteen different theories or models of personal relationships that were then available in the scientific literature. I examined these with the lens of temporal context. I looked at relationships evolving over time in three timeframes: through specific daily *interactions*, which influenced and were influenced by *situations*, which evolved across *phases*. While the dissertation taught me the importance of how personality gets expressed over time depending on the situation, this "bigger picture" of temporal context taught me that we cannot understand the self by studying only personality.

KEY INSIGHT

Life is a mandala that we are woven into and are weaving at the same time. We can attune to this weaving and find and renew intimacy every day.

When we open the aperture on time, we realize that every interaction (meeting, conversation, task) we have with another person is embedded within some type of situation (work, family, travel, conflict, harmony), which is also embedded in some phase of growth, maintenance, or decline. And all of this keeps changing. We are inextricably woven together in a nest of contexts.

Time and Transpersonal Intimacy

With the encouragement of Steve Duck, an expert in the field of personal relationship research, I accumulated more insights into how relationships not only change over time but also how intimacy—a deep knowing and insight into oneself and others—also relates to time. I published this in *Time and Intimacy: A New Science of Personal Relationships*. I wanted to subtitle the book *A Transpersonal Science of Personal Relationships*, but it was decided that name would have limited its marketability. By "transpersonal," I was referencing the *wholeness* I mentioned throughout most books of the QfP collection and above in describing the murmuration. I saw intimacy as a spiritual discipline, the practice of relating to both oneself and another person over time, while attuning to or coming back again and again to this wholeness.

In *Time and Intimacy*, I described the four Radiant Forces—Form (gravity), Chaos (entropy), Time Shaping (cause and effect), and Nurturing Conditions. Intimacy, specifically transpersonal intimacy, emerges from the interplay of these forces. It is important to note that Chaos is an integral part of the cosmic energies that Lilly described. Temporal context is not just a mental construct, a way of looking at the world; it is an inherent part of who we are as human beings relating to each other.

The research indicated that romantic partners go through certain stages and phases over time (they Form). They also interact, schedule, and pace their relationship, moving it into the future (they Time Shape). And, as my thesis showed, they don't always make it; they experience breakups, come together again, or move in and out of friendship, sexual, and commitment phases (they contend with Chaos). I even found one research paper where the idea of Nurturing Conditions clicked into this scheme of temporal context.

In 1991, Hui-Ching Chang and G. Richard Holt explained that yŭan is a chief force that allows contextual factors to play a role in determining whether relationships will work out. "Chinese will often say, 'I have yŭan with another person,' meaning conditions are right for them to be together," Chang and Holt wrote. Yŭan helped me understand my ego struggle with personal relationships. Along with my meditation practice, I understood that my ego's desires and my anxiety about relationships were both parts of an unfolding context; I could do a better job of trusting that context and my role in it.

KEY INSIGHT

We are part of a pattern connected to other patterns that over time are setting the stage for new patterns to emerge. A great peace can fall over us when we realize that harmony, coherence, and many other treasures emerge from this becoming.

My discovery of yŭan and related concepts led me to label Nurturing Conditions as important as the other three Radiant Forces. Following from the previous insight (life is a mandala), I sensed in my heart and in my bones that context is not an abstract, intellectual idea. It is real, vibrant, and alive. We cannot ever be separate from the range of contexts that make up our lives.

From Time and Intimacy to Attractions

While working on *Time and Intimacy*, I taught college classes on personality and transpersonal psychology at Saint Mary's College in Winona, Minnesota. I continued to amass information on the great diversity of approaches to understanding personality. After *Time and Intimacy* was published, I realized that the concepts were too academic and theoretical to be useful to my students. I thought a personality questionnaire would help people grasp these ideas.

At the time, there were a few measures of time orientation in the research literature, including the Zimbardo Time Perspective Inventory, measures of time competence from Shostrom's measure of self-actualization, and the Temporal Inventory on Meaning and Experience (TIME) questionnaire, among others. My goal was not to review all this literature and come up with some new measure. I wanted an easy way to start conveying the four Radiant Forces in a more personal and accessible manner. These previous measures gave me a starting place.

Because of my interest in spirituality, I sent my book to Stephen Kiesling, the editor of the magazine *Spirituality & Health*. I included a summary of my ideas along with a brief essay I had written on preciousness (see *QfP Book 2*, chapter 3). Steve provided helpful feedback. After a few conversations, I was able to translate my ideas into a short article that we coauthored for the magazine. This was published with the title "Navigating in Time" in the 2001 Winter issue, a very auspicious time in the world, just around the time of the attacks of September 11. This was the first time I presented the QFPI™ in a publication and received several letters from readers who shared that they enjoyed it.

Since then, dozens of individuals have taken the more complete version of the QFPI™ shown in this book and through workshops, coaching, and in the course, "The Quest for Presence." In all this work, I have discovered that people do not think about their orientation toward time. When they do, they often touch into something that is beyond their personality. The research literature in psychology tends to overemphasize personality traits, ideas about type, or consistent ways that human beings express character. However, the less time I spend in research, the more I directly experience people needing time out, a method for getting away from fixed notions of personalities, and an opportunity to just be present with each other.

Popular psychology, with the emphasis on traits, has reified the ego to the point where many become more obsessed with their type, styles, strengths, color, and emotional intelligence (EQ) and less attuned to the folding and unfolding of this precious happening life.

KEY INSIGHT

We are all and ever becoming. We just need
to take some time out to see it.

✣ It should have been obvious, but if I followed the thread from one segment to the next, it was inevitable that I would develop the model of Attractions. Everything comes together: my interest in personality, in time, in relationships, in quantum science, and—most of all—in human potential and development of consciousness.

✣ The whole sequence reveals an attraction to something that moved me beyond my past and my earlier and limiting self. I now know that everyone is—at some level—doing the same thing. It may not be in the intellectual sphere of life. It could be social, emotional, spiritual, or through work, a career, a profession, an occupation; or through close, personal relationships with a partner or a spouse. We are all and ever becoming. We just need to take some time out to see it.

Final Reflection

The journey I just described represents an Attraction toward life and away from the anxiety of *having* to show up to life. I know for certain that I would not have been able to make the journey without the help of all my teachers, guides, and supporters, only some of whom I have mentioned here. The thirty years of friendship and love of my wife, Jan, following many years of struggle in previous relationships, has been the most effective catalyst for me to show up and be present.

Different meditation teachers, therapists, coaches, and friends have helped me find ways to transmute my neediness and anxiety into a positive resource. I think human beings will always cycle between a duality of moving toward and moving away from the present moment. This cycle can be called approach and avoidance, attachment and aversion, or "Be here now" and "Be here later."

Many people think about whether they are in one of these two states. They get so excited and almost clamor to be here now. I prefer to think "be in your life" and let completely go of having to be in the now. I now think "be here now" is overrated. It is more effective to see the whole of life as happening forward and backward as well as now. It is all part of the precious weave of Attractions.

Is it really all about practicing mindfulness, gratitude, awe, compassion, and even love? I don't think so. My learnings about essence, field theory, relationship dynamics, yǔan, and temporal context point to a different set of openings. We are here because we will ever be attracted to this unfolding life. For me, a lot of the time was first spent making sense of my anxiety. Gradually, I saw the context—my childhood, conflict, relationships, attachment—that situated my anxiety as part of a much bigger purpose. Eventually, I transmuted that anxiety into positive learning. Today, I have had students who take my classes tell me that they don't have to be anxious anymore.

We grow in the process of *moving into and through* each of the unfoldings; we know to avoid getting too caught up in any one way that we might show up to life. We live by visiting with and listening to others who help us along the different paths of this movement. We love by embracing the vulnerability, the essence, of all of us moving together; it is a wonderful thing when we find ourselves along whatever path is attracting us. For, in the end, we are grateful for that initial fear or pain—or anxiety—that first pulled us into looking.

Using the QFPI™ with Workplace Teams

I work in the field of organizational wellness, helping workplaces develop practices that support employee well-being. Whenever possible, I like giving the QFPI™ to groups of coworkers for team-building or as part of a workplace retreat. It is always helpful to view Attractions in the context of those with whom we work. You can also use the QFPI™ with any group (e.g., families, sports teams, church, or synagogue).

Below is one example that illustrates how groups may influence the expression of one's Attraction and how any individual may serve a particular function for the group depending on their Attraction. This graph shows the results from twenty employees who provide community services to parents as part of outreach and education for a large metropolitan school district. My organization conducted a team-building and "vision" retreat for the group to help with recent organizational changes and prepare for the new school year.

As can be seen in the diagram on the following page, many on the team have their Attraction *toward* the lower right corner, between the areas of Centering, Synthesizing, and Intending. For this brief case study, I will focus on three individuals who fell toward the group's periphery. Specifically, see the dotted line surrounding those who are (a) on the outside edges of the dots and (b) farthest away from the center of the group and Synthesizing.

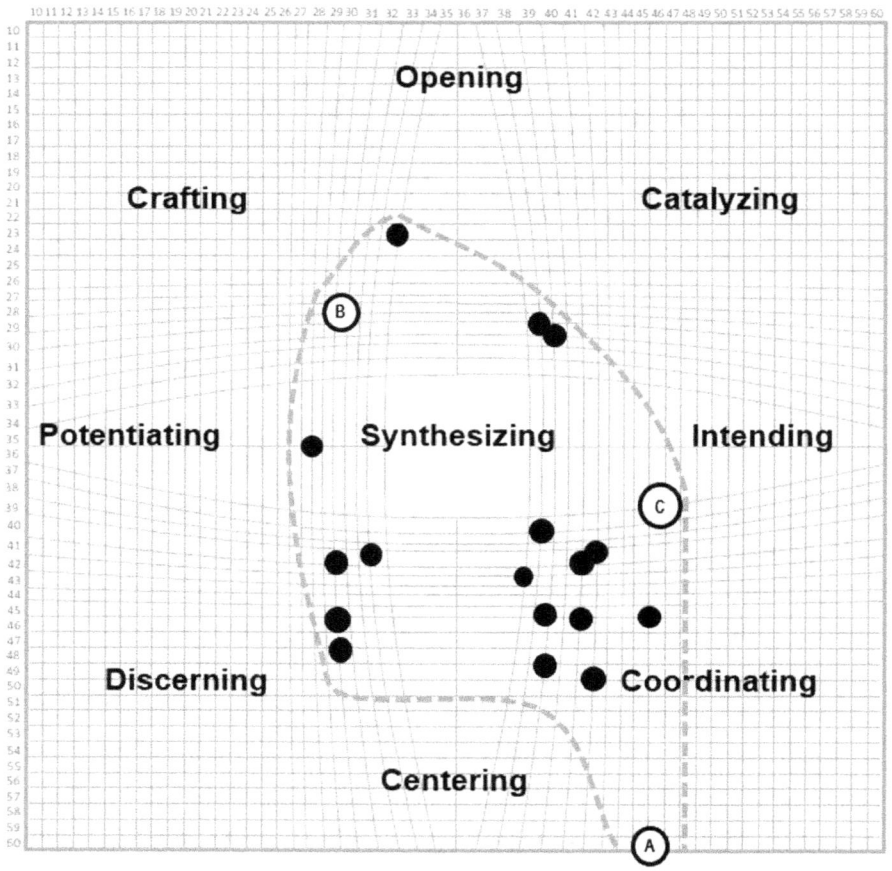

Person A. Obviously, this employee scored the most extreme on the vertical dimension possible, clearly pointing to their Attraction as Centered with some Coordinating as well. Interestingly, this person was the key administrative assistant and central office coordinator for the entire team. Their tendency to be organized was also apparent, given their behavior during the retreat. They had organized all the food, schedule, rosters, and other materials and were known as the "go-to" person—the "bedrock" that everyone could turn to for resources and logistics. In the context of all others, this administrative assistant served a "centering" function for the team. They "knew" everyone, and everyone knew where this person was.

Person B. This employee scored toward Synthesizing. However, in the context of the group and relative to others, they had a higher Attraction to Crafting with some Potentiating. This employee was in a higher management or "director" role and, unlike most others, did a lot of family outreach and community coordinating and spent much of their time exploring and building connections. Much of their conversation focused on possibilities and potential, bringing out the team's strengths. They were less concerned with the day-to-day work and more with the vision of services for the community. They served a "potentiation" function in the context of all others. They helped encourage the team's potential in the direction of a positive vision.

Person C. In the context of the group and relative to others, this employee had the greatest leaning toward Intending. Throughout the retreat, they were relatively quiet. However, when participating in group tasks, they focused on what needed to be done and the ability to contribute. They served primarily to act, to do what was required. It would be minimizing to say that this person was a "gopher"—an informal term that refers to a person whose job is to do small tasks for others. Their Intending or "Time Shaping" orientation was a deeper willingness to serve the group.

Groups are dynamic systems that live in a space of Attraction. The process above—of using the QFPI™ to reflect on dynamics—allows me, on an intuitive level, to see the big picture. I may discern how groups tend toward the same or different areas or how individual players complement the team.

During the retreat, I asked everyone to share why they felt they are the way they are. Participants not only expressed what they have in common (a sense of community) but also how they are unique and how their unique style helps the group. I asked team members to recognize each other for their unique contributions. Seeing how people feel validated and not judged for their essential Attractions is very satisfying. In addition, I have an intuitive sense of the "health" of a team when I see too much uniformity (clustering) in one area. I also spoke with the team's director and suggested ways to bring people who are outliers (persons A, B, and C) together.

Key Terms

Attraction. In our Quest for Presence, Attraction has two interrelated meanings.

1) Attraction refers to our distinctiveness, the unique tendencies that each person has toward life, well-being, and higher states of aliveness, fulfillment, actualization, and transcendence. Every human being is preprogrammed with a drive, a striving, to experience higher states of consciousness. However, there are individual and subjective differences in the expression of this drive. These differences also vary from day to day and across the lifespan.

2) Attraction refers to our entire state of being as an organic and dynamic human system that is constantly adapting to life. We are a whole "mind-body-spirit" system. Attraction is an objective process by which this system self-organizes into this wholeness or coherence, or makes modifications or adapts to maintain, sustain or re-create such order whenever there is some change. Outside of clock-time, our deepest experiences of time emerge from self-organization and adaptation. We learn about our own distinctiveness, our unique tendencies (definition 1) from adaptation (definition 2). As we gain insight into our unique tendencies, we also learn about the coherence of the system.

Attractions or *Nine Attractions*. The nine Attractions represent personal tendencies that each individual has toward one or more of the four Radiant Forces. Attractions show us how our particular attitudes, moods, motives, and strengths move (pull, draw, invite) us from our current state of being to a deeper, more essential, or soulful state, one that is more in touch with the Radiant Forces. In contrast to personality, which often refers to an outer self, persona, or mask, Attractions refer to an inner potential to realize the forces within our own being.

Attractor. The concept of an attractor is borrowed from modern theories of chaos and complexity (also see Research Notes from Chapter 1). In our Quest for Presence, an attractor refers to the four Radiant Forces on our journey through time, the dynamic and ongoing pull of those forces on the expression of our self and soul while on that journey. The four Forces operate like attracting magnets and move us in time, through time, and beyond time. They actively shape our most intimate experience of time.

Attraction Matrix. In biology, a matrix is an environment or material in which something develops, a surrounding medium or structure. In mathematics, a matrix is a collection of numbers arranged into a fixed number of rows and columns. The Attraction Matrix combines these two definitions. A matrix is both a "slice" in time, a symbolic representation (mathematics), and a "dynamic unfolding" or actual expression of life (biology). Symbolically, it refers to the graphic representation of the four Radiant Forces and the nine Attractions. This is depicted graphically on page 45 and is provided to help guide, locate, and get our bearings in working with metaphysical concepts. In actuality, the matrix refers to the time-space dance and configuration of the forces as they influence our lifelong experiences, growth, and development.

Enfolding. Refers specifically to the process of bringing or incorporating *information* from and through the journey of life. There are different types of information: 1) new information from the external world; internal sensations, thoughts, and intuitions; and memory traces; 2) inklings, inspirations, aspirations that are born from our soul or essence; and 3) momentary or continuous experiences of transcendence—the Treasures (see *QfP Book 5*). We do not simply take this information in like input into a computer. Instead, our personalities are themselves an ongoing and dynamic manifestation of these enfoldings. There is another definition of enfolding that points to our future, most fulfilled, or purposeful self—the fullest realization of our potential. This self exists outside time and is pulling our current personality toward it. As we, however haphazardly, move toward that realized self, the occasions of our life give us information. This information is enfolded in our journey.

Levels of Attraction. Quest for Presence distinguishes three levels of Attraction. Level 1 refers to feelings and motives that cause us to approach the "other"—another person, place, object, goal, or event. This is the most commonly used version of the verb, attract (lowercase a) as in "I am drawn to or attracted to him" or "We felt a pull to visit the little village in the countryside." Level 2 refers to Attraction as a "state of being" that can manifest continuously or in this very moment. Level 1 Attraction refers to some external other (person, thing, place, event) that will manifest in the future as we act toward that other. Level 2 refers to an internal experience that may or may not involve action as much as devotion, intuition, contemplation, inner work, or spiritual longing. Level 3 refers specifically to the operation of the four Radiant Forces as they influence and are influenced by our own quest for presence. There is a whole and varied set of Attractions that live beyond our personal or egoic attraction to the "other" or to a "state." This whole set of Attractions is shaping, forging, and molding our entire journey and life story. Awareness of, and attunement to, Level 3 Attraction involves developing the Soulful Capacities (*QfP Book 2*) and understanding our own personal Attractions (see definition above for *Attractions or Nine Attractions*).

Personality (also outer self, persona, mask). As defined here, personality refers to a set of traits and qualities that distinguishes how a person appears unique or would be characterized as unique by others. Personality is distinct from one's more inner-self, essence, or soul.

Radiant Forces. The fundamental or deep source of the precious weave and discussed in depth in *QfP Book 1*. The forces are specifically forces *of time*; that is, everything that happens and that we experience *as happening* emerges or unfolds through the activity of these forces. Each force is itself energy and strength with the potential to move things, influence, and provide power, ultimately causing our experience to unfold. Our experience of time's Flow (moving from past to present to future) also depends upon the operation of each force and its influence on each of the others. These forces exist independently of our experience, but we would not have an experience without them.

Temporal Context. In my book *Time and Intimacy*, I list fourteen different definitions of temporal context. For purposes of *QfP Book 3*, this is defined as the living medium within and through which all the various threads of time's precious weave cohere and evolve together: the Radiant Forces, Soulful Capacities, the Attractions, the Trajectories, and the Treasures. Temporal context is most likely to be experienced through the force of Nurturing Conditions.

Unfolding. Technically, to unfold means to reveal, disclose, open, or spread out something that is in a folded position. This technical definition reveals two aspects of the action of unfolding: probability and position. Anything that moves from a folded to an unfolded position or state is moving through certain phases that are more probable than other phases. Our Quest for Presence is itself an unfolding where we realize there is no such thing as position. Position is only a slice, an illusion that clock-time reifies. Hence, unfolding means that the Radiant Forces (beyond clock-time) are revealing themselves as we move from moment to moment or phase to phase in our journey.

Research Notes

(page 6) **A new paradigm is emerging.** The term *paradigm* refers to a pattern of methods, ideas, theories, and perspectives that scientists tend to agree are the prevailing way of understanding the things they study. Perhaps the most popular model of personality in modern psychological research is the Five-Factor Theory (FFT) developed by McCrae and Costa (1996). In an early formulation of FFT, they clearly indicate *dynamic* processes take place between five "layers" of personality: basic trait tendencies, the ways human beings adapt, self-concept, objective biography, and external influences. Despite the central role of these dynamics, they recently noted, "The research record remains compartmentalized, focusing on one layer at a time with too little attention to the developmental dynamics of interactions among layers" (Costa, McCrae, and Löckenhoff, 2019). That this limitation exists, despite twenty-five years of research, suggests that the paradigm is not working. It is unclear what a new paradigm will look like. The current QfP approach assumes that it is the dynamics themselves—the processes, the unfolding of our life—that are central. It is not the layers but the weave, the dynamic relationships *over and through time* between the layers. For potential clues inside the academic field of psychology, interested readers may read the work of Dan Gilbert on the power of time (Gilbert et al., 2002 and Gilbert, 2014), the powerful role of experience and neuroplasticity on changing personality (Davidson, 2001), and studies showing that personality isn't permanent (Hardy, 2020) or "set in stone" (Zaraska, 2021). Other authors speak to what some label as pseudoscience: applying quantum physics and cosmology to models of the self. Sometimes, what is currently seen as "pseudo" science becomes the paradigm. Time will tell.

Costa, P. T., Jr., McCrae, R. R., & Löckenhoff, C. E. (2019). Personality across the life span. *Annual Review of Psychology, 70*, 423–448. https://doi.org/10.1146/annurev-psych-010418-103244

Davidson, R. J. (2001). Toward a biology of personality and emotion. *Annals of the New York Academy of Sciences, 935*(1), 191–207. https://doi.org/10.1111/j.1749-6632.2001.tb03481.x

Dixon, R. D., Jr. (2017, October 11). *What quantum physics can tell you about your identity*. Medium. https://medium.com/the-mission/how-quantum-physics-freed-my-identity-16a96e6f4a7c

Gilbert, D. (2014, March). *The psychology of your future self* [Video]. TED Conferences. https://www.ted.com/talks/dan_gilbert_the_psychology_of_your_future_self

Gilbert, D. T., Gill, M. J., & Wilson, T. D. (2002). The future is now: Temporal correction in affective forecasting. *Organizational Behavior and Human Decision Processes*, 88(1), 430–444. https://doi.org/10.1006/obhd.2001.2982

Hardy, B. P. (2020). *Personality isn't permanent: Break free from self-limiting beliefs and rewrite your story*. Portfolio/Penguin.

Harth, E. (2008). The element of time in the emergence of mental phenomena. *Journal of Consciousness Studies*, 15(4), 54–65. https://www.ingentaconnect.com/contentone/imp/jcs/2008/00000015/00000004/art00003

Laszlo, E. (2014). *The self-actualizing cosmos: The akasha revolution in science and human consciousness*. Inner Traditions.

McCrae, R. R., & Costa, P. T., Jr. (1996). Toward a new generation of personality theories: Theoretical contexts for the five-factor model. In J. S. Wiggins (Ed.), *The five-factor model of personality: Theoretical perspectives* (pp. 51–87). Guilford Press. https://psycnet.apa.org/record/1996-97942-003

Roth, P. (2008). *Indignation*. Houghton Mifflin Company.

Zaraska, M. (2021, August 19). *Scientists once thought personality was set in stone. They were wrong*. Discover. https://www.discovermagazine.com/mind/scientists-once-thought-personality-was-set-in-stone-they-were-wrong

Zohar, D., & Marshall, I. N. (1990). *The quantum self: Human nature and consciousness defined by the new physics*. William Morrow & Co.

(page 7) To reify or not to reify—on reification. Generally, to reify means to make something (seem or appear) concrete or real when it may not actually be real. In psychology, reify has three uses relevant for our Quest for Presence: 1) only seeing what we want to see, 2) acting toward others in ways that lead them to act in a certain way, and 3) taking our self to be more fixed than it actually is. First, *confirmation bias* is the tendency for human beings to unwittingly and unconsciously only look for, select, and believe in information that confirms preexisting beliefs (Nickerson, 1998). Second, research on the *self-fulfilling prophecy* (*expectancy-confirmation bias* or *Pygmalion effect*) indicates that what we believe to be true will become true (get fulfilled), so much so that teachers who believe students are smart will behave toward them in ways that, under certain conditions, actually result in those students getting better grades (Madon et al., 1997). The key phrase in that last sentence was "under certain conditions." As human beings, we have the ability to adjust our situation and not fall prey to cognitive biases (Jussim, 2012). Third, mindfulness meditation practice seeks to de-reify our own self-concept. Human beings have a proclivity for "perceiving momentary experiences as events, then portraying them as objects which seem to exist through time. We tend to use nouns, rather than verbs." This alternative view in Buddhist psychology claims that "The self which we perceive as a unity is merely a collection of processes—conditioned reactions to what the person has experienced" (Mamberg & Bassarear, 2015). Reification also can occur in society as a whole (Honneth, 2008). For purposes of this book, it is important to recognize that while personality traits can endure over time (See first

Research Note for page 6 above), reification is a significant factor behind that endurance, and it is possible to bring awareness and de-reify the self.

Honneth, A. (2008). *Reification: A new look at an old idea.* Oxford University Press.

Jussim, L. (2012). *Social perception and social reality: Why accuracy dominates bias and self-fulfilling prophecy.* Oxford University Press.

Madon, S., Jussim, L., & Eccles, J. (1997). In search of the powerful self-fulfilling prophecy. *Journal of Personality and Social Psychology, 72*(4), 791–809. https://doi.org/10.1037/0022-3514.72.4.791

Mamberg, M. H., & Bassarear, T. (2015). From reified self to being mindful: A dialogical analysis of the MBSR voice. *International Journal for Dialogical Science, 9*(1), 11–37. https://vc.bridgew.edu/psychology_fac/79

Nickerson, R. S. (1998). Confirmation bias: A ubiquitous phenomenon in many guises. *Review of General Psychology, 2*(2), 175–220. https://doi.org/10.1037/1089-2680.2.2.175

CHAPTER 1

(page 12) On Attraction. One meaning of "attraction" used in this book refers to our being drawn or pulled onto some path of personal or spiritual development, a journey of presence. Subsequent paragraphs in this chapter explain Attraction in more detail. It is important to distinguish these ideas from the concept of the "law of attraction" or what may be labeled as manifestation metaphysics. In physics, Newton's law of universal gravitation states that gravity is an attractive force and that every mass attracts every other mass. In "New Age" or "New Thought" philosophy, the law of attraction states that positive thoughts (affirming, uplifting, and inspirational thinking) can and will eventually produce positive experiences in our life and, similarly, negative thoughts bring about negative experiences. The associated dictum is "Change your thinking, change your life." Attraction, as used in *QfP*, refers to how human beings—as complex, self-organizing systems or "selves"—are attracted to certain forces. One of these forces is gravity (in line with Newtonian physics). Another force is Nurturing Conditions, or the very biopsychosocial context of our own evolution and becoming. This idea of Attraction comes more from complexity and chaos theory. "Attraction can be understood as the process by which a system self-organizes into coherence and adapts to maintain, sustain or recreate such order when subject to change either from internal functioning or external influence" (Pryor & Bright, 2007). We are always—at some level and often difficult to discern—self-organizing on a path of development. This is our Attraction to the Quest for Presence. Regarding coherence, in *QfP Book 5 (The Treasures)*, you can learn about how coherence is something we can experience as one of life's treasures. Also, please see the Key Terms section of this book for definitions of Attraction, Attractions, and Attraction Matrix.

Pryor, R. G. L., & Bright, J. E. H. (2007). Applying chaos theory to careers: Attraction and attractors. *Journal of Vocational Behavior, 71*(3), 375–400. https://doi.org/10.1016/j.jvb.2007.05.002

(page 13) **Remember that our personality is not our essence or soul—on remembering.** The use of the term *remember* does not refer to our memory of our past (episodic memory) or of things that we previously learned or associated, as in remembering a skill or language. Here, to remember means to recollect our soul, our essence, or our inherent wholeness (see *QfP Book 2*). The philosopher George Gurdjieff described "self-remembering" to mean that we make the daily effort to remain conscious of who we are, where we are, and what we are doing as opposed to acting on automatic. There is no thought; one is just alive to what is happening. This is the essence of presence. Many human beings believe that they are conscious and aware. They believe that they are their personality, but they lie to themselves. That is, they act as though they are not influenced by various cognitive biases (see above Note 1 for page 6) or reification (Note 2) or attractive forces (Note 3). To remember is to stay vigilant to these forces and to cultivate more Soulful Capacity (see *QfP Book 2*).

Needleman, J., & Baker, G. (Eds.). (1998). *Gurdjieff: Essays and reflections on the man and his teachings*. Continuum.

Ouspensky, P. D. (2001). *In search of the miraculous: Fragments of an unknown teaching*. Harcourt, Inc.

(page 14) **Fragments of self.** Having, maintaining, or finding a sense of self and identity as *one coherent whole being* is an essential part of Quest for Presence. Most paths of development (spiritual, psychological, personal) draw a distinction between one's whole or true self and one's divided, false, shadow, or lost self. This is not a strict dichotomy or black-and-white difference. Fragmentation—in and of itself—is not a negative, evil, or dark force. It may have been caused by unconscious and immoral acts. Only some examples are given here. Twelve-step programs for recovery from addiction describe *character defects*. The psychologist Carl Jung described *ego complexes* as unconscious or repressed aspects of oneself that are split off from the self. The dominant concept of "sin" in Christianity refers to doing things that separate us from the divine, to fall from grace, to do evil. We can also fixate on certain aspects of our personality as more important to our sense of self than others (*ego fixation*). Each path offers a way toward wholeness, either through self-inventory, trust in a higher power, forgiveness, redemption, therapy, journaling, group work, or any number of meditative practices. Human beings can have these fragments or shadows and still maintain or work toward a sense of oneself as having a coherent identity. However, under severe trauma or extreme stress, it is possible to develop dissociative identity disorder, where we feel we don't own parts of ourself. Fragmentation is more likely with a background involving adverse childhood experiences (ACES), such as shame, abuse, neglect, exposure to violence, rage, and caregivers with serious mental illness or narcissism. It is possible to heal and recover from even these situations.

Danese, A., & McEwen, B. S. (2012). Adverse childhood experiences, allostasis, allostatic load, and age-related disease. *Physiology & Behavior*, *106*(1), 29–39. https://doi.org/10.1016/j.physbeh.2011.08.019

Ogawa, J. R., Sroufe, L. A., Weinfield, N. S., Carlson, E. A., & Egeland, B. (1997). Development and the fragmented self: Longitudinal study of dissociative symptomatology in a nonclinical sample. *Development and Psychopathology, 9*(4), 855–879. https://doi.org/10.1017/S0954579497001478

Stav, O. S., Mikulincer, M., & Sharabany, R. (2021). Studying self-fragmentation from Kohut's self psychology perspective: Development and validation of the Fragmented Self Inventory. *Psychoanalytic Psychology, 38*(1), 39–48. https://doi.org/10.1037/pap0000309

Zweig, C., & Abrams, J. (Eds.). (1991). *Meeting the shadow: The hidden power of the dark side of human nature.* Jeremy P. Tarcher/Penguin.

(pages 15-16) Box 1.1: Attractors. The metaphor of the empty box with equidistant magnets is taken from the use of the term "attractor" in theories about chaos and complexity. To illustrate, let's assume that the human self is a complex system that has, over time, states of relative stability and relative instability. We are always in some transition between these states. In other words, we experience this happening life as inherently *transient.* After something happens in our life (our biography, our story, our narrative), we generally return to or are moved to another state of relative stability or instability. An attractor is whatever our entire system behaves like after it passes through a transient state. There are different types of attractors. Some are labeled *limit cycle,* which means a system that cycles periodically over the same set of states, never coming to rest. In contrast, *strange attractors* describe more chaotic systems where a system never returns to the same exact state. It lacks a periodic or cyclical shape. Various researchers in the field of health suggest that human beings—and our behaviors and physiology—are healthier when approached more like a chaotic system. That is, some systems behave erratically, have built-in unpredictability, and functions that may "split-off" and act autonomously from the whole (see previous Note on fragments of self). Instead of treating human beings as simple linear systems that behave in simple ways, we may learn more from exploring the different attractors and complexities.

Plsek, P. E., & Greenhalgh, T. (2001). The challenge of complexity in health care. *BMJ, 323*(7313), 625–628. https://doi.org/10.1136/bmj.323.7313.625

Resnicow, K., & Page, S. E. (2008). Embracing chaos and complexity: A quantum change for public health. *American Journal of Public Health, 98*(8), 1382–1389. https://doi.org/10.2105/AJPH.2007.129460

Rickles, D., Hawe, P., & Shiell, A. (2007). A simple guide to chaos and complexity. *Journal of Epidemiology & Community Health, 61*(11), 933–937. http://dx.doi.org/10.1136/jech.2006.054254

(page 16) Definition of entropy from Brian Greene. Brian Greene is a popular science writer and has hosted several television shows about the cosmos and quantum mechanics. The quote is from a recent book that explores how, out of chaos, human thought came to exist in the cosmos, and the purpose of life and the mind. The quote reflects a key principle that Greene elucidates, which he calls the "entropic two-step." The book explains that the force of evolution leads to evolving complexity—what we call the force of Form—and the truth of entropy—what we label the force of Chaos—which are fundamental. "The entropic two-step and the evolutionary forces of selection enrich the pathway from order to disorder with prodigious structure, but whether stars or black holes, planets or people, molecules or atoms, things ultimately fall apart" (Greene, 2020).

Greene, B. (2020). *Until the end of time: Mind, matter, and our search for meaning in an evolving universe.* Alfred A. Knopf.

(page 19) Change your biology: Enfolding and your genetic template. The idea that we have the ability to change our personalities and that personality traits are not completely fixed was described above in Note 1 for page 6. The new science of epigenetics also suggests that biology is not destiny. To a certain extent, how our genes get expressed in our behavior depends on our lifestyle and, in turn, our lifestyle can have an impact on our genes. Studies show that only a small fraction of personality traits are due to heritability or DNA (Weaver, 2022). Dr. Kenneth Pelletier explains that our habits and thoughts play a significant role in our wellbeing and suggests meditation, diet, and exercise can significantly reprogram our genetic expression. Pelletier argues that "change your gene, change your life" is a new reality facing the human species. Compare with the Note on Attraction above ("Change your thinking, change your life.").

Pelletier, K. R. (2018). *Change your genes, change your life: Creating optimal health with the new science of epigenetics.* Origin Press.

Weaver, I. (2022). Epigenetics in psychology. In R. Biswas-Diener & E. Diener (Eds.), *Noba textbook series: Psychology.* DEF Publishers. Retrieved from http://noba.to/37p5cb8v

(page 20) Your intuition is essential. The ideas expressed in previous Research Note entries may make no sense to you. Perhaps you think more concretely about data, life, and experience. A new paradigm? Reification? Attraction? Remembering? You don't find these ideas very useful. If so, I encourage you to use your intuition. The contemplations and exercises in this book are provided as much to help you awaken or enrich your intuition as to give you a personal anchor for the ideas. One way to look at this journey into your personality and Attractions is what Emily Sadowski calls *intuition development pedagogy* (IDP), which is a coherent synthesis and program of practices that already exist. Contemplation plays a central role in IDP, but so do meditation, creativity, imaginative play, dreamwork, all forms of introspection, and use of symbolic imagination, to name a few. For now, just trust that something is unfolding that will awaken, unlock, uncover, and reveal another thread or layer of this precious weave and your destiny.

Sadowski, E. R. (2017). *Intuition and intuition development: Practices for the inner self.* [Doctoral dissertation, Simon Fraser University]. Simon Fraser University Summit Research Repository. https://summit.sfu.ca/item/17780

Emily Sadowski's website: http://www.emilysadowski.com/ and her (2023) book *What Is Intuition? Resonance. Connection, and Trusting Intuition on its own Terms* from One Can Press (Ontario, Canada).

(page 20) Most people believe in the Soul. *QfP Book* 2 provides more depth on this research (see Research Notes in Chapter 2 in *QfP Book* 2, specifically for pages 20 and 21).

(page 22) Relational knowing and process consciousness. Relational knowing, sometimes associated with feminist approaches or "women's ways of knowing," starts from the assumption that everything we have ever learned or will learn comes from the need for connection to others and occurs in the context of peers and social engagements and the overall frame of our relationships over time. Process consciousness is more complex to define. Essentially, human beings have the ability to experience themselves as they receive sensations in a continuous state, to experience Flow and to let go and live in the process of life (Schaef, 1992). Our attention and awareness are not only discrete but also continuous (Herzog et al., 2020). We can be aware at each single point in time (continuous, as in watching a movie) as well as conscious only at certain moments of time. Process consciousness is strengthened when we are in touch with the Soulful Capacities of Acceptance, Presence, Flow, and Synchronicity (see *QfP Book 2*). The view of personality put forward here rests more on relational knowing than merely content knowledge (formal-book-informational-skill) and more on process than discrete (digital-just now) consciousness.

Belenky, M. F., Clinchy, B. M., Goldberger, N. R., & Tarule, J. M. (1986). *Women's ways of knowing: The development of self, voice, and mind.* Basic Books.

Csikszentmihalyi, M. (1990). *Flow: The psychology of optimal experience.* Harper & Row.

Herzog, M. H., Drissi-Daoudi, L., & Doerig, A. (2020). All in good time: Long-lasting postdictive effects reveal discrete perception. *Trends in Cognitive Sciences,* 24(10), 826–837. https://doi.org/10.1016/j.tics.2020.07.001

Schaef, A. W. (1992). *Beyond therapy, beyond science: A new model for healing the whole person.* HarperCollins.

CHAPTER 2

(pages 31–33) Box 2.1: Toward a Dynamic View of the Self: Self-Construal and Construal-Level Theory. This note, along with initial Research Notes 1 and 2 above (New Paradigm and Reification), may be combined together as a comment on research that may support the Attractions model. Specifically, our self can change; we can engage in the world in ways that do not reify our (previous) self-concept; we can construe a new self (projected into the future) in ways that are diverse and agile; and we can realize our successful future self. The wealth of research on independent and interdependent self-construal stems from Markus and Kitayama (1991), one of the most cited articles in the field of psychology and also Cross and Madson (1997). DeCicco and Stroink (2007) launched the more recent study of metapersonal self-construal. Construal-level theory is based on the work of Trope, Liberman, and Wakslak (2007). The diverse findings that I synopsize in this section come from other studies listed below. The most interesting among these is the work of Chan and Saqib (2022). Results across four studies indicate that an individualistic orientation or independent self-construal results in feeling that events take longer and that this appears due to arousal and the need for arousal that comes with agency or having to take action. In contrast, those with an interdependent orientation may feel less time compression in ordinary or calming conditions. Other articles cited provide diverse perspectives for interested readers.

Readers interested in DeCicco and Stroink's metapersonal measure should review Chapter 9 (The Temple) in *QfP Book 2* on the Soulful Capacities and the list of eleven different measures of spiritual health and self-transcendence. I am not aware of any study that has compared any or all of these with metapersonal self-construal. However, as conceived here, the Soulful Capacities and Attractions play off of and nourish each other. The Soulful Capacities provide the rich ground for the experience of spiritual health while on our journey. In contrast, the Attractions are what push and pull us along the journey. Gradually, as we contemplate what is happening, we construe our "self" as having greater and greater (metapersonal) capacity for the expression of our soul nature in life. At the same time, Acceptance, Presence, Flow, and Synchronicity give us the capacity to contemplate.

Chan, E. Y., & Saqib, N. U. (2022). How long has it been? Self-construal and subjective time perception. *Personality and Social Psychology Bulletin, 48*(4), 624–637. https://doi.org/10.1177/01461672211016919

Cross, S. E., & Madson, L. (1997). Models of the self: Self-construals and gender. *Psychological Bulletin, 122*(1), 5–37. https://doi.org/10.1037/0033-2909.122.1.5

DeCicco, T. L., & Stroink, M. L. (2007). A third model of self-construal: The metapersonal self. *International Journal of Transpersonal Studies, 26*(1), 82–104. https://digitalcommons.ciis.edu/cgi/viewcontent.cgi?article=1353&context=ijts-transpersonalstudies

Hardin, E. E., Leong, F. T. L., & Bhagwat, A. A. (2004). Factor structure of the self-construal scale revisited: Implications for the multidimensionality of self-construal. *Journal of Cross-Cultural Psychology, 35*(3), 327–345. https://doi.org/10.1177/0022022104264125

Heller, D., Stephan, E., Kifer, Y., & Sedikides, C. (2011). What will I be? The role of temporal perspective in predictions of affect, traits, and self-narratives. *Journal of Experimental Social Psychology, 47*(3), 610–615. https://doi.org/10.1016/j.jesp.2011.01.010

Markus, H. R., & Kitayama, S. (1991). Culture and the self: Implications for cognition, emotion, and motivation. *Psychological Review, 98*(2), 224–253. https://doi.org/10.1037/0033-295X.98.2.224

Morseth, B. K. (2016). *The self-transcendent existential present: Empirically examining the behavioral implications and relationships between mindfulness, self-construal, and mortality salience.* [Master's thesis, University of California, Santa Barbara]. https://alexandria.ucsb.edu/downloads/vh53ww07m

Norasakkunkit, V., Kitayama, S., & Uchida, Y. (2012). Social anxiety and holistic cognition: Self-focused social anxiety in the United States and other-focused social anxiety in Japan. *Journal of Cross-Cultural Psychology, 43*(5), 742–757. https://doi.org/10.1177/0022022111405658

Perunovic, W. Q. E., & Wilson, A. E. (2009). Subjective proximity of future selves: Implications for current identity, future appraisal, and goal pursuit motivation. In K. D. Markman, W. M. P. Klein, & J. A. Suhr (Eds.), *Handbook of Imagination and Mental Simulation* (pp. 347–358). Psychology Press.

Takano, K., Sakamoto, S., & Tanno, Y. (2011). Ruminative and reflective forms of self-focus: Their relationships with interpersonal skills and emotional reactivity under interpersonal stress. *Personality and Individual Differences, 51*(4), 515–520. https://doi.org/10.1016/j.paid.2011.05.010

Terblanche-Greeff, A. C., Dokken, J., van Niekerk, D., & Loubser, A. R. (2018). Cultural beliefs of time orientation and social self-construal: Influences on climate change adaptation. *Jàmbá: Journal of Disaster Risk Studies, 10*(1), Article a510. https://doi.org/10.4102/jamba.v10i1.510

Trope, Y., Liberman, N., & Wakslak, C. (2007). Construal levels and psychological distance: Effects on representation, prediction, evaluation, and behavior. *Journal of Consumer Psychology, 17*(2), 83-95. https://doi.org/10.1016/S1057-7408(07)70013-X

Wegemer, C. M. (2020). Selflessness, depression, and neuroticism: An interactionist perspective on the effects of self-transcendence, perspective-taking, and materialism. *Frontiers in Psychology, 11*, Article 523950. https://doi.org/10.3389/fpsyg.2020.523950

(page 37) From Arthur Deikman. Deikman's book is a seminal description of the aspect of our minds that can observe events as they unfold without conceptualization or automatic reactivity. We have the ability to take our own thoughts as ephemeral objects that come and go. This is also the basis of much mindfulness meditation practice. As described here, the Attractions are not attachment experiences that we seek, desire, or try to obtain as though they would give us pleasure. Instead, we just notice what states we are attracted to as reflections of the Radiant Forces. There is a detached quality. Deikman's work is cited and developed more by the work of Steven Hayes and colleagues in a therapeutic methodology called Acceptance and Commitment Therapy.

Bennett, J. B. (2014). *Raw coping power: From stress to thriving.* Organizational Wellness & Learning Systems (OWLS). https://organizationalwellness.com Available at Amazon https://www.amazon.com/Raw-Coping-Power-Stress-Thriving/dp/0991510208

Deikman, A. J. (1983). *The observing self: Mysticism and psychotherapy.* Beacon Press. (quote from pp. 94–95).

Hayes, S. C., & Smith, S. (2005). *Get out of your mind and into your life: The new acceptance and commitment therapy.* New Harbinger Publications.

(page 38) Reading chapter 1 before taking the survey. Quest for Presence is designed with the intent that the reader can enter into any book at any time and not necessarily read each book in sequence. Trust your intuition. You can dive into the QFPI™ or you can wait. You may benefit from just reading chapter 1. In the case of the Attractions, it may help some readers to review Q*f*P Books 1 and 2, to see the greater context of how the Forces work (Book 1) and how the Attractions dance with the Soulful Capacities (Book 2).

CHAPTER 3

(page 54) Joseph Campbell quote is from the *Joseph Campbell Companion*, which contains many great insights. Please check it out: https://www.jcf.org/

(page 85) Quote for Contemplation (Q*f*P 3-3): Jennings, K. (2012). *Maphead: Charting the wide, weird world of geography wonks.* Scribner.

CHAPTER 6

(page 116) Insights on marriage and social perception. There is an extensive body of research on how accurately we perceive others and our ability to understand or empathize with them. It is beyond the scope of this book to even summarize this literature. However, in everyday human interaction people tend to have automatic ("snap") judgments of others rather than deliberative or heedful review of data and their perceptions are subject to many biases (see Note 2 for page 7 above). As intimacy develops, and within close relationships and marriage, both familiarity with and accuracy of partners' emotions, attitudes, and views appear related to greater relationship satisfaction. Added to this is a sense of differentiation, feeling more autonomous and interdependent than dependent. Partners who better differentiate themselves from each other may also be more satisfied. I believe that the QFPI™ can be useful for improving accuracy as well as differentiation.

Ambady, N., Bernieri, F. J., & Richeson, J. A. (2000). Toward a histology of social behavior: Judgmental accuracy from thin slices of the behavioral stream. *Advances in Experimental Social Psychology, 32,* 201–271. https://doi.org/10.1016/S0065-2601(00)80006-4

Clark, M. S., Von Culin, K. R., Clark-Polner, E., & Lemay, E. P., Jr. (2017). Accuracy and projection in perceptions of partners' recent emotional experiences: Both minds matter. *Emotion, 17*(2), 196–207. https://doi.org/10.1037/emo0000173

Ickes, W. (1993). Empathic accuracy. *Journal of Personality, 61*(4), 587–610. https://doi.org/10.1111/j.1467-6494.1993.tb00783.x

Kenny, D. A., & Acitelli, L. K. (2001). Accuracy and bias in the perception of the partner in a close relationship. *Journal of Personality and Social Psychology, 80*(3), 439–448. https://doi.org/10.1037/0022-3514.80.3.439

Peleg, O. (2008). The relation between differentiation of self and marital satisfaction: What can be learned from married people over the course of life? *The American Journal of Family Therapy, 36*(5), 388–401. https://doi.org/10.1080/01926180701804634

Sanbonmatsu, D. M., Uchino, B. N., & Birmingham, W. (2011). On the importance of knowing your partner's views: Attitude familiarity is associated with better interpersonal functioning and lower ambulatory blood pressure in daily life. *Annals of Behavioral Medicine, 41*(1), 131–137. https://doi.org/10.1007/s12160-010-9234-0

CHAPTER 7

(page 121) de Beauvoir and Sartre. Interested readers might wish to read these in-depth treatments:

de Beauvoir, S. (2013). *Adieux: A farewell to Sartre.* Pantheon.

Rowley, H. (2005). *Tete-a-tete: The tumultuous lives and loves of Simone de Beauvoir and Jean-Paul Sartre.* Harper.

(page 122–123) Discovering essence. These Lilly and Naranjo books helped start me on my journey.

Lilly, J. C. (1972). *The center of the cyclone: An autobiography of inner space.* Julian Press, Inc.

Naranjo, C. (1972). *The one quest.* Viking Press.

(page 125) Research on the Enneagram. At the time I learned of it, there was nothing published about the Enneagram. Over the past forty years, there have been hundreds of books, courses, and workshops devoted to understanding the Enneagram. A few authors (A. H. Almaas, Sandra Maitri, Joseph Howell, Christopher Heuertz) place personality in the context of its origin in the cosmic forces of the Holy Ideas. Others clearly discuss the distinction between personality and essence with guidance on how to work in developing essence (Helen Palmer, Don Richard Riso, Russ Hudson). Most books and workshops focus on assessing the nine personality styles and types, understanding associated blind spots, seeing the neuroses, and working with these for personal growth. While this appears helpful, I have not found any research to show that study of the Enneagram in this way actually improves psychological health, self-actualization, or self-transcendence. References below suggest few, if any, studies that validate the existence of types.

Godin, J. (2010) *The effect of the Enneagram on psychological well-being and unconditional self-acceptance of young adults* (Publication No. 11816) [Doctoral dissertation, Iowa State University]. ISU Digital Repository. https://doi.org/10.31274/etd-180810-2243

Komasi, S., Soroush, A., Nazeie, N., Saeidi, M., & Zakiei, A. (2016). Enneagram personality system as an effective model in prediction of risk of cardiovascular diseases: A case-control study. *Journal of Cardio-Thoracic Medicine,* 4(3), 468-473. https://doi.org/10.22038/JCTM.2016.7403

Sutton, A. (2012). "But is it real?" A review of research on the Enneagram. *Enneagram Journal,* 5, 5–20. Access here: https://e-space.mmu.ac.uk/583471/ or Access here: https://ieaninepoints.com/wp-content/uploads/2019/01/2012-IEA-Journal_Anna-Sutton.pdf

(page 126) Neurotheology. This science has grown some since my 1976 undergraduate thesis. The science of neurotheology involves theories and studies that seek to understand religious and spiritual experiences in terms of neuroscience, brain studies, and psychophysiology. As applied to Quest for Presence, neurotheology would seek to understand the specific neurological correlates of the Soulful Capacities, the Attractions, and the experience of the Treasures. For example, scientists have begun to study the neural basis of the experience of some of the Treasures (Awe, Savoring, Spontaneity; see *QfP Book 5*) and the Flow state.

Guan, F., Xiang, Y., Chen, O., Wang, W., & Chen, J. (2018). Neural basis of dispositional awe. *Frontiers in Behavioral Neuroscience,* 12, Article 209. https://doi.org/10.3389/fnbeh.2018.00209

Heisenberg, W. (1958). *Physics and philosophy: The revolution in modern science.* Harper & Brothers.

Saggar, M., Quintin, E. M., Kienitz, E., Bott, N. T., Sun, Z., Hong, W., Chien, Y., Liu, N., Dougherty, R. F., Royalty, A., Hawthorne, G., & Reiss, A. L. (2015). Pictionary-based fMRI paradigm to study the neural correlates of spontaneous improvisation and figural creativity. *Scientific Reports,* 5, Article 10894. https://doi.org/10.1038/srep10894

Speer, M. E., Bhanji, J. P., & Delgado, M. R. (2014). Savoring the past: Positive memories evoke value representations in the striatum. *Neuron, 84*(4), 847–856. https://doi.org/10.1016/j.neuron.2014.09.028

van Elk, M., Gomez, M. A. A., van der Zwaag, W., van Schie, H. T., & Sauter, D. (2019). The neural correlates of the awe experience: Reduced default mode network activity during feelings of awe. *Human Brain Mapping, 40*(12), 3561–3574. https://doi.org/10.1002/hbm.24616

Yoshida, K., Sawamura, D., Inagaki, Y., Ogawa, K., Ikoma, K., & Sakai, S. (2014). Brain activity during the flow experience: A functional near-infrared spectroscopy study. *Neuroscience Letters, 573*, 30–34. https://doi.org/10.1016/j.neulet.2014.05.011

(page 128) **Morning anxiety.** I now wonder whether morning anxiety is a "threshold symptom." It is biofeedback from our mind-body system telling us that we are not yet ready to be present to life, that we are still adjusting to growing up and being "all-in" to this happening life. The transition from dream-to-wake is a microcosm of our own lifelong transition to waking. Since my first study in 1976, there has been more systematic research on anxiety and neuroticism and some research on morning anxiety as well. Two things stand out in this literature that also relate to the concept of emerging adulthood (i.e., the transition from adolescence to adulthood). First, most of the literature on waking anxiety examines it primarily within the context of nightmares and dreams. That is, some people, perhaps especially in adolescence, have waking anxiety because of sleep and not because of their personality. Second, studies show that neuroticism is linked to both depression and anxiety, and in dynamic ways across phases of adolescence (Nelemans et al., 2014).

Coolidge, F. L., Segal, D. L., Coolidge, C. M., Spinath, F. M., & Gottschling, J. (2010). Do nightmares and generalized anxiety disorder in childhood and adolescence have a common genetic origin? *Behavior Genetics, 40*(3), 349–356. https://doi.org/10.1007/s10519-009-9310-z

Jylhä, P., & Isometsä, E. (2006). The relationship of neuroticism and extraversion to symptoms of anxiety and depression in the general population. *Depression and Anxiety, 23*(5), 281–289. https://doi.org/10.1002/da.20167

Nelemans, S. A., Hale, W. W., III, Branje, S. J. T., Raaijmakers, Q. A. W., Frijns, T., van Lier, P. A. C., & Meeus, W. H. J. (2014). Heterogeneity in development of adolescent anxiety disorder symptoms in an 8-year longitudinal community study. *Development and Psychopathology, 26*(1), 181–202. https://doi.org/10.1017/S0954579413000503

Simor, P., Köteles, F., Sándor, P., Petke, Z., & Bódizs, R. (2011). Mindfulness and dream quality: The inverse relationship between mindfulness and negative dream affect. *Scandinavian Journal of Psychology, 52*(4), 369–375. https://doi.org/10.1111/j.1467-9450.2011.00888.x

(page 129) **Brain lateralization of emotion.** I trained twenty female subjects in a guided visualization technique. They were asked to recall, visualize, and feel emotions associated with adjectives that were previously rated as highly positive (example: loving), negative (hateful), or neutral (methodical). Their task was to apply these adjectives to themselves and let feelings emerge. I knew this was working, not only from the ratings of the subjects but also because many of them cried spontaneously during the tasks. When asked, their tears were as much about tenderness and care as they were about feeling sadness or grief.

At the time of my undergraduate work, several studies suggested that the right frontal lobes were associated with more negative emotional experiences and the left frontal lobes were associated with positive emotional experiences. Electroencephalograph (EEG) studies have since shown that emotion-related disturbances, such as depression and anxiety, have been linked to relative right-sided resting frontal EEG asymmetry (Thibodeau et al., 2006). Functional MRI studies have shown that greater left-sided activity is observed for approach emotions like love, happiness, pleasance, and humor, whereas right-sided neural activity is associated with negative/withdrawal emotions like sadness, anxiety, and anger. (Murphy et al., 2003). More recent meta-analysis suggests that brain regions associated with the experience of emotion are the same as those associated with receiving any signal from our *viscera* (internal organs) (Lindquist et al, 2016). The following quote (with citations removed) from Lindquist and colleagues is based on their meta-analysis of 397 functional magnetic resonance imaging (fMRI) and positron emission tomography studies (containing 914 experimental contrasts and 6827 participants).

They claim that certain brain regions are: "routinely engaged not just when people experience an affective feeling but even in so-called cognitive states when internal sensations in the body, including afferent signals and central nervous system representations, are used to guide the allocation of attention. Given that interoceptive information is the basis of affective feeling and changes across a wide range of mental states, this finding is consistent with the hypothesis that *every conscious moment has some affective tone; circuitry within the affective workspace may infuse each and every conscious moment with some degree of positivity or negativity* (italics added for emphasis).

Lindquist, K. A., Satpute, A. B., Wager, T. D., Weber, J., & Barrett, L. F. (2016). The brain basis of positive and negative affect: Evidence from a meta-analysis of the human neuroimaging literature. *Cerebral Cortex*, 26(5), 1910–1922. https://doi.org/10.1093/cercor/bhv001

Murphy, F. C., Nimmo-Smith, I., & Lawrence, A. D. (2003). Functional neuroanatomy of emotions: A meta-analysis. *Cognitive, Affective, & Behavioral Neuroscience*, 3(3), 207–233. https://doi.org/10.3758/cabn.3.3.207

Thibodeau, R., Jorgensen, R. S., & Kim, S. (2006). Depression, anxiety, and resting frontal EEG asymmetry: A meta-analytic review. *Journal of Abnormal Psychology*, 115(4), 715–729. https://doi.org/10.1037/0021-843X.115.4.715

Citation for my undergraduate thesis. Davidson, R. J., Schwartz, G. E., Saron, C., Bennett, J., & Goleman, D. J. (1979). Frontal versus parietal EEG asymmetry during positive and negative affect. *Psychophysiology*, 16, 202–203.

(page 130) Affective Style. Affective style generally refers to a broad range of individual differences in specific features of emotional responding. The science is progressing from understanding how the brain works during emotional experiences, including right-left differences and other brain regions, to postulating how people can be trained to utilize this information to improve their well-being.

Coan, J. A., & Allen, J. J. B. (2004). Frontal EEG asymmetry as a moderator and mediator of emotion. *Biological Psychology, 67*(1–2), 7–50. https://doi.org/10.1016/j.biopsycho.2004.03.002

Dahl, C. J., Wilson-Mendenhall, C. D., & Davidson, R. J. (2020). The plasticity of well-being: A training-based framework for the cultivation of human flourishing. *Proceedings of the National Academy of Sciences, USA, 117*(51), 32197–32206. https://doi.org/10.1073/pnas.2014859117

Davidson, R. J. (2004). Affective style: Causes and consequences. In J. T. Cacioppo & G. G. Berntson (Eds.), *Essays in social neuroscience* (pp. 77–91). MIT Press.

(page 131) Insights from Master's Thesis—citation for my presentation. Bennett, J. (1982). *The changing nature of interpersonal processes. A model for viewing interdependence in and over time.* [Paper presentation]. International Conference on Personal Relationships, Madison, WI, United States.

(page 133) Need for power. Because of my "time" experience with the master's thesis, I wanted to study how these different needs expressed themselves in behavior over time. We conducted an experiment where we brought participants together to have a discussion to reduce conflict in a group. Participants varied in their need for power and influence. Trained research assistants observed these participants through a one-way mirror as they engaged in the group-task. These observers rated the participants on various behaviors, such as attempts at dominance (such as raising their voice) and releasing tension (such as laughter). We saw another pattern emerge. Without going into detail, the results of the experiments I ran made it clear that the previous ratings of power and influence predicted how participants behaved. Those with a stronger need for power, which was more "ego" driven (correlating with narcissism), clearly showed less of a tendency to care about the outcomes of the group and more about asserting themselves.

Following from my initial studies, several research studies have used the need for power/need for influence measure and concepts. A number of studies focuses on the relationship between power and narcissism (e.g., Alexander et al., 2020). Others take a more deliberate view, finding that perceived ability influence correlates with well-being (Sommer & Bourgeois, 2010), and that male and female managers differ in their needs and abilities.

Alexander, M. B., Gore, J., & Estep, C. (2020). How need for power explains why narcissists are antisocial. *Psychological Reports, 124*(3), 1335–1352. https://doi.org/10.1177/0033294120926668

Bennett, J. B. (1988). Power and influence as distinct personality traits: Development and validation of a psychometric measure. *Journal of Research in Personality, 22*(3), 361–394. https://doi.org/10.1016/0092-6566(88)90036-0

Kocur, D., & Mandal, E. (2018). The need for power, need for influence, sense of power, and directiveness in female and male superiors and subordinates. *Current Issues in Personality Psychology*, 6(1), 47–56. https://doi.org/10.5114/cipp.2018.72200

Sommer, K. L., & Bourgeois, M. J. (2010). Linking the perceived ability to influence others to subjective well-being: A need-based approach. *Social Influence*, 5(3), 220–244. https://doi.org/10.1080/15534510903513860

(page 137) Yǔan, Time and Transpersonal Intimacy—reference for Chang and Holt. I discuss yǔan in much more depth in my book *Time and Intimacy*.

Bennett, J. B. (2000). *Time and intimacy: A new science of personal relationships.* Routledge.

Chang, H.-C., & Holt, G. R. (1991). The concept of yuan and Chinese interpersonal relationships. In S. Ting-Toomey & F. Korzenny (Eds.), *Cross-cultural interpersonal communication* (pp. 28–57). Sage Publications, Inc. https://psycnet.apa.org/record/1991-97471-002

(page 138) Zimbardo and measures of time orientation. Below is a sample of references. This is a great starting place.

Block, R. A., Saggau, J. L., & Nickol, L. H. (1984). Temporal inventory on meaning and experience: A structure of time. *Imagination, Cognition and Personality*, 3(3), 203–225. https://doi.org/10.2190/8R3N-3UGJ-K2JK-PE9R

Boyd, J. N., & Zimbardo, P. G. (1997). Constructing time after death: The transcendental-future time perspective. *Time & Society*, 6(1), 35–54. https://doi.org/10.1177/0961463X97006001002

Shostrom E. L. (1964). An inventory for the measurement of self-actualization. *Educational and Psychological Measurement,* 24(2), 207–218. https://doi.org/10.1177/001316446402400203

Yonge, G. D. (1975). Time experiences, self-actualizing values, and creativity. *Journal of Personality Assessment*, 39(6), 601–606. https://doi.org/10.1207/s15327752jpa3906_10

Zimbardo, P. G., & Boyd, J. N. (1999). Putting time in perspective: A valid, reliable individual-differences metric. *Journal of Personality and Social Psychology*, 77(6), 1271–1288. https://doi.org/10.1037/0022-3514.77.6.1271

Acknowledgments

This is the tale of two journeys: My own story and also the story of the Quest for Presence collection itself. Throughout the books in the QfP collection, I acknowledge many teachers, friends, and family for their contribution to my story. For those personal acknowledgements, I direct readers to the books, especially Chapter 7 in Book 3.

But the story of this entire Quest for Presence—the many who helped birth it, and its many phases—all began with several opportunities to share early ideas. Thanks to Dr. Steve Duck, Lawrence Erlbaum Press published *Time and Intimacy: A New Science of Personal Relationships* in 2000. These were research and academic ideas. I yearned to have more practical conversations and started searching. I was first graced with the open arms of the C. G. Jung Society of North Texas (thank you, Maureen Lumley), Unity Church of Dallas and also of Fort Worth, Magellan Healthcare, and also Brandeis University (thank you, Marci McPhee), all of whom brought me in to conduct workshops or retreats in 2000 and early 2001. These offerings had titles like "The Quest for Presence: Time & the Transformation of Work," "Time & Intimacy: Finding Serenity in a Busy World," and "Time and the Soul's Journey." Positive reactions from many participants suggested my ideas had personal relevance.

Around that time, I sent a copy of *Time and Intimacy* to the then-editor of *Spirituality & Health* magazine, Stephen Kiesling. Steve was a key to everything that came next. Through several great conversations, he helped me to reimagine my early drafts of the Quest for Presence Inventory™ (QFPI™). Thanks to Steve for publishing "Navigating in Time" in his magazine in the Winter 2002 issue. I received some calls from readers of that article. One, in particular, was a book-store owner who encouraged me to write a book.

I also continued to offer workshops, especially at the National Wellness Institute (NWI) in Stevens Point, Wisconsin. I also delivered a train-the-trainer workshop at NWI on "Time and Spiritual Health." Then, the Center for Substance Abuse Prevention (CSAP) at the Substance Abuse and Mental Health Services Administration (SAMHSA) provided further support. Because of a CSAP research grant, between 2002 and 2004 I was able to deliver "Time and Spiritual Health" to employees at small businesses in the Dallas-Fort Worth Metroplex as part of a randomized clinical trial. I especially want to thank Dr. Deborah Galvin, who helped me navigate the grant application and implementation process.

This research study made the concepts even more real. My colleagues (from the Recovery Resource Council in Fort Worth) and I taught "Time and Spiritual Health" to employees in diverse occupations, including car wash attendants, construction workers, engineers, employees in a manufacturing plant, school bus drivers, university administrators, teachers, and physical plant staff. When results from our research with these "everyday" people showed improvements in well-being, I knew these ideas were no longer just academic concepts. Thanks to Richard Sledz, Camille Patterson, Kelly Heath, Wyndy Wiitala and the whole team who helped to implement this study. Thanks to Shawn Reynolds for getting these research findings published.

The many conversations with dozens of these early colleagues and students laid the foundation for the next phase of this work. I am grateful to them and apologize for not mentioning them all. This next phase began with writing. The first draft of *Quest for Presence* was actually a single book. I asked Sandra Wendel (of Write On, Inc.), the editor for my previous book, *Raw Coping Power: From Stress to Thriving,* to start editing. Instead, Sandy suggested I first have a group of beta readers provide feedback. She recommended approaching individuals who were familiar with my work as well as others who did not know me.

This five-book Quest for Presence collection emerged as a result of the in-depth, honest, and very insightful feedback from twenty beta readers. Sandy received the feedback anonymously but separately shared the names of reviewers. I am grateful to Sandy for her ongoing guidance (then and now) and to each and every one of the reviewers: Art Wimberly, Briane Agostinelli, Cassie Menn, Cynthia Conigliaro, Gary Loper, Heather Sittler, Heidi Postupack, Janette Helm, Jaymee Spannring, Katharine Hunter, Kimberly Gray, Laura Anne Crowder, Michele Studer, Paul Feather, Rachel Kopke, Regina Novak, Rose Whitcomb, Sadie Liller, Sandy Kogut, and Teresa Przetocki. I also appreciate input from Faith Geiger, Rachael Baker, Janet DeLong and many others who I likely have forgotten. Oh, Wait! Special thanks to Kimberly Gray for always reminding me about the quantum "popping in."

These reviewers were given a list of almost twenty questions, providing a structure for their reactions to the book. Nonetheless, I was overwhelmed with the sheer amount and detail of feedback—almost 20,000 words and over forty pages. My colleague Shelby Pittman combed through the data searching for common words and themes. Her analysis revealed that readers were excited about the content but overwhelmed by the complexity and depth of the ideas. Importantly, they wanted to retain all the key features of the book; for example, the spiritual message, the odes, the contemplations, and my own story. Many suggested that several books and a separate workbook would make the quest easier to digest. Shelby helped me take the next step to start restructuring the book.

At the same time, I had started teaching virtual courses of "The Quest for Presence." The students who took the class also helped me further refine ideas, and several contributed their QFPI™ profiles (see Book 3). These students included Anissa Amason, Briane Agostinelli, Laura Anne Crowder, Cynthia Conigliaro, Tracey Cox, Madge Cruse, Tyler Currier, Melanie DuPon, Shahinaz Elhennawi, Kristie Ellison, Brenda Fister, Kimberly Gray, Deborah Hamlin, Susan Hansen, Mark Head, Lucy Hoblitzelle, Kathleen Klug, Lindsay Levin, Michele

Mariscal, Jennifer Markley, Jocelyne Maurice, Wesley Miller, Renee Moy, Alan Porzio, Sazha Ramos, Desiree Reynolds, Sandy Salvo, John Shelton, Stephany Sherry, Andy Siegle, John Steakley, Michele Studer, Zac Tolbert, Melanie Weinberger, Art Wimberly, and Susan Yenzer. Thank you for your presence.

Throughout this process, I have been most grateful to those contributing a "treasure story" (see Book 1 and Book 5). This includes a number of people already mentioned, as well as Kathy Carlton, Sara Christopher (Acker), Michaela Conley, and John Weaver. Thank you for reminding me that the Treasures are real and true.

Repackaging a single document into multiple volumes and a workbook was daunting. I want to thank Shelby again for her help. Also, Aldrich Chan went through manuscripts, collated all the research references, and found the proper citations for the hundreds of research notes found at the back of every book. Both Shelby's and Aldrich's responsiveness to my requests was a tremendous aid that kept me going.

The final phase of this story was guided by my editors. First, thanks to Sue Hansen of Duck Sauce Life for her exquisite detail in meaningful developmental reviews. Sue's questions, along with her own personal insights, helped me to further clarify ideas in substantive rewrites. Candace Johnson took these edited drafts and, with great thoughtfulness, helped to refine final drafts. Thank you, Sue and Candace, for your patient and thorough work.

Special thanks go to others who helped with design: Gary Rosenberg (from The Book Couple) for beautiful interior design and book covers, Jeffrey McQuirk for his ideas and patience in rendering the images of the four Radiant Forces, and my dear friend Ellen McCown for her gentle spirit and suggestions for artwork.

At the start of this acknowledgment section, I refer readers to reading the books to find acknowledgments of people in my personal life. I also have to give special thanks to my friends Art Wimberly, Spencer Seidman, and Cynthia Conigliaro—each of whom spent many hours listening to me ramble on and on about my struggles as a writer on this quest of time. Their playful feedback helped me feel so much less alone during periods of dismay and doubt. Thanks, guys!

Finally, I could say that none of this would have been possible without the love, support, and kindest patience of my wife, Jan. The truth is, I could have pulled off some of it … maybe. However, I know it would not be anything approaching the rich tapestry that I hope readers see through so many words. My own ability to see this tapestry—of the preciousness of this life and my love of life—comes from Jan. She, more than anyone I have ever known, lightens me, gives me confidence, and so makes it possible for me to listen more and listen deeply. I am so grateful for her and our many years together.

About the Author

Joel Bennett, PhD, is president of Organizational Wellness & Learning Systems (OWLS), a consulting firm that specializes in evidence-based wellness and e-learning technologies to promote organizational health and employee well-being. Dr. Bennett first delivered stress management programming in 1985, and through the efforts of over 400 resilience facilitators and coaches who have been trained in OWLS' evidence-informed curriculum as well as consulting in South Africa, Italy, and Brazil, OWLS programs have since reached over 250,000 workers across the United States and internationally. OWLS has received over $6 million in National Institutes of Health funding for workplace well-being research, and their programs have been recognized as effective by independent bodies, including the US Surgeon General.

OWLS consults on Integral Organizational Wellness™ approaches that combine leadership, champion, team, and peer-to-peer strategies: nudging the true culture of health. Joel is the author of 50 peer-reviewed research articles and chapters and has authored or coauthored eight books, including *Heart-Centered Leadership* (with Susan Steinbrecher), *Raw Coping Power: From Stress to Thriving*, *Your Best Self at Work* (with Ben Dilla), and *Well-Being Champions: A Competency-Based Guidebook*, *Time and Intimacy*, *Preventing Workplace Substance Abuse*, and *The Connoisseur of Time*.

Dr. Bennett has served in advisory and board roles for various organizations including Magellan Health; Aetna; the National Wellness Institute; It's Time Texas, Work Healthier Advisory Committee; the Academy of Management Division on Management and

Spirituality; the Global Wellness Institute; the International Foundation of Employee Benefits Plans; and the State of Texas Primary Prevention Planning Committee (Preventing Sexual Violence).

In 2022, he received the William B. Baun Lifetime Achievement Award from the National Wellness Institute for his contributions to the professional field of wellness. He also received the Positive Leadership Award from the Positive Leadership Institute for forward-thinking management practices that help employees, teams, and organizations thrive.

Joel lives in North Texas with Jan, his wife of twenty-eight years, and around the corner from his wonderful son, daughter-in-law, and grandchildren, who call him "Obi." He hopes that one day he will become a Jedi Knight or something.

www.ingramcontent.com/pod-product-compliance
Lightning Source LLC
Chambersburg PA
CBHW060516130626
46553CB00002B/514